Mark Rathe

D0017263

Man
of Faith

Man of Faith

Learning from the life of Abraham

RAY C. STEDMAN

MULTNOMAH · PRESS

Portland, Oregon 97266

Unless otherwise identified, all Scripture references are from the Revised Standard Version of the Bible, copyright 1946, 1952, © 1971, 1973, Division of Christian Education, National Council of the Churches of Christ in the U.S.A. Used by permission.

Cover design by Phil Malyon and Judy Quinn
Photograph by Wayne Aldridge

MAN OF FAITH
© 1986 by Ray C. Stedman
Published by Multnomah Press
Portland, Oregon 97266

Published in cooperation with Discovery Foundation,
Palo Alto, California

Printed in the United States of America

All rights reserved. No part of this publication may be reproduced, stored in a retrieval system, or transmitted, in any form or by any means, electronic, mechanical, photocopying, recording, or otherwise, without the prior written permission of the publisher.

Library of Congress Cataloging-in-Publication Data

Stedman, Ray C.
    Man of Faith.

    1. Abraham (Biblical patriarch)—Meditations.
    2. Bible. O.T. Genesis IX, 27-XXV, 8—Meditations.
    I. Title.
    BS580.A3S75   1986   222'.110924   85-21772

    85 86 87 88 89 90 91 – 10 9 8 7 6 5 4 3 2 1

CONTENTS

1
THE BEGINNING OF FAITH

(Genesis 11:31-12:9)

There is a simple secret that ties together the Old and the New Testaments and makes the study of the Old Testament a never-ending delight. The Old Testament is designed as a picture book, illustrating with fascinating stories the spiritual truths presented in the New Testament. This is especially true of the books of Moses (Genesis through Deuteronomy) and the book of Joshua; for in the life histories of men like Abraham, Jacob, and Moses, we have symbolized for us the progress of spiritual growth.

One of the most convincing proofs of the inspiration of the Bible is how the Spirit of God has taken simple history—facts as they were lived out day by day—and recorded them in such a way as to weave an accurate pattern of the development of spiritual life. What took place physically in the Old Testament is a spiritual picture for contemporary believers of what takes place in their own growth in grace.

It is not mere fancy to view the Old Testament in this manner; the New Testament itself gives ample proof that God planned the structure of his book in just this way. In the tenth chapter of 1 Corinthians, Paul refers to many incidents in the history of Israel. He concludes the account with these words:

> *Now these things happened to them as a warning (literally "type"), but they were written down for our instruction, upon whom the end of the ages has come (1 Corinthians 10:11).*

And in Romans 15:4, he says,

> *For whatever was written in former days was written for our instruction, that by steadfastness and by the encouragement of the scriptures we might have hope.*

The letter to the Galatians, as well as our Lord's own use of these stories, further shows they were regarded as an analogy to the course of intended spiritual development.

We need, of course, to guard against wild and fanciful interpretations. We must move with care so that we do not overstep the laws of interpretation. But it would be a pity to miss (for example) Old Testament illustrations of the great Christian truths reflected in the book of Romans and elsewhere. Abraham's life beautifully portrays justification by faith; Isaac teaches us what it means to be a son, a child of God; Jacob's life is designed to show us how God works in sanctification to deliver us from the reigning power of sin; and Joseph is a stunning picture of what it means to be glorified by resurrection and thus enter into the challenging and exciting task that awaits the final unveiling of the sons of God.

Perhaps the clearest and most helpful of all these Old Testament portraits is the record of Abraham's life, beginning in distant Ur of the Chaldees and ending at last in the cave of Machpelah near Hebron, in Canaan. Abraham is clearly the model man of faith. Again and again in the New Testament he is held up as *the* example of how God works in the life of a man to fulfill his promises of grace. He is obviously chief of all the heroes of faith recorded in Hebrews 11. And in addition to the Christian faith, two of the great religions of the earth hold him in high esteem.

Therefore we may well begin the study of this man's life with a sense of excitement. In Abraham we will find ourselves reflected. In tracing his life's story we shall discover the very secrets by which the Spirit of God intends to transform us from faltering pilgrims into men and women of stalwart faith, worthy to stand beside the heroes of Hebrews 11.

Abraham is first introduced to us in the closing verse of Genesis 11 and in the opening verses of Genesis 12. His name was originally Abram; it was not until years later that it was changed to Abraham. The reason for this change was highly significant, and we shall examine it in due course. But for now let us get acquainted with young Abram. The Spirit of God passes over his early life in Ur of the Chaldees with but the briefest notice, and begins the sacred record with his encounter with God. This is where life truly begins!

We know from Stephen's great speech (recorded in the seventh chapter of Acts) that this call came to Abraham when he lived in Ur of the Chaldees. It was once thought that Ur was a very primitive city. I have read several books which attempt to depict Abram as an ignorant, unlettered nomad of the desert who lived in a primitive mud-walled village. We could hardly expect to find in such a man much more than the primitive search of a barbarian struggling to discover God. But the spade of the archaeologist has since turned up the ruins of Ur, and we have learned that this was a city of great wealth and considerable culture, containing a library and a university. The city was devoted to the worship of the Moon Goddess, and it is almost certain that Abram was an idolater, a worshiper of the moon. The book of Isaiah more than hints at this.

Stephen declared that the God of glory appeared to Abram there in Ur. We have no knowledge of the form this appearance took. But whatever it was, it is important to note that *God took the initiative*. This is true throughout history. Men may think they are feeling after God, but that feeling itself is the drawing of a seeking God. Here then is God, suddenly breaking into the life of Abram as he lived in Ur, worshiping the moon and kneeling before his dumb idols.

In this meeting Abram came face to face with a command and a promise; he was commanded to go, and he was promised a land. There is no question that the land to which he was to go was a literal place. Likewise the promise to make his name great and to make him the father of many nations has been literally fulfilled. I stress this now because I am not going to mention it again in this study. I believe in the literal fulfillment of these promises as history has already amply confirmed them. The study of how God literally fulfilled these to Abram is helpful and illuminating; but our concern here is to discover another dimension in this historical account. We will follow the warrant given to us by the New Testament, and make spiritual application to our own lives of what we see here.

Above all, we must not make the mistake (which is so common today) of taking these promises of the Old Testament and applying them literally to the believer today. When Israel, for instance, was told that they were not to intermarry with other races, God meant what he said. But when we try to apply that literally to nations today, we get into all sorts of absurdities. Some of the false concepts on which the doctrine of racial segregation is based come from an attempt to apply the instructions of God to Israel in a literal way today. We must not follow that road.

Still, all these things were written for our spiritual instruction. As we read this great command and promise to Abram, we may see ourselves here. For this is nothing more nor less than what God says to every person today, in a spiritual sense.

Abram was commanded to do three things: leave his country, his kindred, and his father's house. This is exactly the command that comes to every person who hears the call of the gospel today. We are to leave our country—the place where we have been living, our residence since birth. That is not our physical residence, but rather the old life with all its ambitions, loyalties, worship of money and fame and power, its imagined independence which is really slavery—all that we have been by nature since birth. There comes a command in the gospel to leave our country. This is a picture of the world—organized society with its satanic philosophies and value systems.

Abram was also told to leave his relatives. In the spiritual sense these are the moral forces that shape

our lives. Just as blood relatives affect us greatly on
the physical level, so these moral forces at work today
change our lives constantly and color all that we
think and do. The opinions of others, the traditions
of men, the pressures from family and friends, the attitudes of our employers and others around us—these
are the kindred we must be willing to forsake when
we hear the call of God. When God confronts us with
his call, these cannot count any longer. We are to renounce all concern about what others think and be
preeminently concerned about what God thinks.

Third, Abram was to leave his father's house—
that is, the ties with the "old man." Our father, in
this sense, is Adam, the father of us all. What theolo-
gians call our "Adamic nature" is the father's house
in which we all live. We are called to leave this, no
longer putting any dependence upon our looks, tal-
ents, or any of our normal resources. Instead we must
begin to walk in dependence upon another to do
through us what we cannot do ourselves.

This is where a man stands when he first hears the
gospel. He may have grown tired of the land of Ur,
for it is a land of darkness, of weariness of soul, of
spiritual hunger and death. Yet when the call of the
word of God comes to him, there is much that seems
desirable in the old life. He hesitates to leave, feeling
the pull of these things upon him. Undoubtedly,
Abram felt this hesitancy. The land to which he was
called was unknown. It could not be known until it
was experienced. But he could not deny the reality of
God, and he could not evade the clear command: "Go
from your country and your kindred and your father's
house to the land that I will show you."

Have you heard this command of God in your own
life? Have you heard the living God, the God of
glory, say to you, "You must no longer depend upon

what you have been depending on—the opinions, the attitudes, the philosophy in which you have been reared. These are wrong. They are based upon the lies of Satan and you must not live on this basis any longer. You must learn to accept the truth reflected in the Word of God, though it cuts right across the philosophy of this world. You must, above all, leave your father's house; that is, dependence upon your "natural self." It is a simple but vital decision—you cannot stay in Ur and go to the land at the same time.

Now with this command comes a mighty promise. It, too, is threefold:

> And I will make of you a great nation, and I will
> bless you, and make your name great, so that you
> will be a blessing. I will bless those who bless you,
> and him who curses you I will curse; and by you
> all the families of the earth shall bless themselves
> (Genesis 12:2,3).

The first promise, that God would make of Abram a great nation, was literally fulfilled in Israel. But what does it symbolize spiritually, to us? What is a *nation*?

It is simply the life of a man, expanded and enlarged to great proportions. In our day, a nation may be made up of a thousand strains from many different family groups, all living together in a heterogeneous society. Such is not the biblical nation. In the Bible, every nation begins with a man; then there is the family, and as the family grows and expands, there is finally the nation. Every nation is but the continued, expanded life of a man.

This promise, then, becomes for us a picture of eternal life, which is the first promise of the gospel. "The wages of sin is death" (that is the old country of Ur), "but the free gift of God is eternal life in Christ

Jesus our Lord" (Romans 6:23). Leave your country, your kindred, and your father's house, and what happens? "I will give you eternal life," God says. "I will make of you a great nation. I will constantly expand and enlarge your life—life will take on infinite proportions for you."

The second promise, "I will bless you and make your name great so that you will be a blessing," meant several specific things to Abram. As we trace the story of his life, we find it meant he would have riches, he would find honor, and he would be a blessing to others. He would become influential and effective.

This is spiritually what God offers today. Of course, if you are thinking of dollars and cents, you are on the wrong track; this is never promised to a believer. God never commits himself to make us wealthy when we become Christians, but he does promise us the riches of Christ. Paul says, "O the depth of the riches and wisdom and knowledge of God! How unsearchable are his judgments and how inscrutable his ways!" (Romans 11:33). These are, indeed, wonderful riches. This is the adventure the world is looking for more than anything else. Men are earnestly looking for something that will satisfy them within and change them without, and they will spend everything for it. But money cannot buy it. Only in Jesus Christ can you become what God intended you to be. Only in Christ can you fulfill the beauty of your womanhood or the glory and strength of your manhood. *These* are the riches of Christ.

But God offers still more—he offers honor (but not the honor of men). If you are looking for big crowds and excitement and the praises of men, you might consider running for political office; but if you are looking for honor, *genuine honor*, then listen to the words of Christ: "If any one serves me, the Father will honor him" (John 12:26b). The honor he will give makes you the very nobility of earth; your name will be listed with those in Hebrews 11:38, "of whom the world was not worthy . . . ."

Last, God offers this, the choicest of all: "I will make you a blessing." This is the glory of being used to bless others, the joy of a fruitful life. There is nothing more wonderful than that. It has been my privilege on a few occasions to have God use my life in a way that has opened up and blessed the hearts of others, and I tell you there is no other joy like it on earth. It is the most thrilling experience to feel that God has used you—the words you have spoken, the things you have said—to solve someone's desperate problem, to make life begin to unfold for them, to see homes reunited, estranged hearts brought together, and problems solved. This is what God offers every believer in Jesus Christ. All these—riches, honor, and blessing—are part of the second promise of the gospel.

But there is yet a third part: "I will bless those who bless you and him who curses you I will curse, for by you all the families of the earth shall be blessed." What is this but the truth of identification, of sonship? It is what every parent thinks of his child: "I will bless those who bless him, and those who curse him I will curse." We are wrapped up in our children. They are the apple of our eye, and whatever touches them touches us. So John writes, "See what love the Father has given us, that we should be called children of God" (1 John 3:1). God says, "I will identify myself with you. What concerns you, concerns me." But listen to this again: "I will bless those who bless you, and him who curses you I will curse." That is, we will be identified with God in the eyes of the world. We will be, like him, a creator of crises. Everywhere you go, you will be either a blessing or a curse . . . but no one will ignore you. God will make your life so vitally in touch with himself that you will have the effect he has when he touches lives.

It was so with Jesus of Nazareth. No one ever came into contact with him and remained neutral. This is what God says to each pilgrim in the life of faith: "If you will leave your country, your kindred, and your father's house, I will make you into this kind of person, so that you will affect every life you touch for better or for worse. They will bless you or they will curse you." Surely this is what Paul means in 2 Corinthians 2:15-16:

> For we are the aroma of Christ to God among those who are being saved and among those who are perishing, to one a fragrance from death to death, to the other a fragrance from life to life. Who is sufficient for these things?

This is God's design for the Christian. Your life will be vibrant with that vitality that God himself possesses. Then all the families of earth will be blessed through you. That is universal usefulness. God will take anyone and touch the world in some sense through him. This is a vast and marvelous promise, is it not? Perhaps now you can see that in these brief, ancient words to Abram, God has hinted about the life detailed in the pages of Romans, Ephesians, Galatians, and Corinthians—in all of the New Testament. It includes all God offers to do in us through Christ.

Note that *it is all of God*. Abram was to do nothing except obey; God would do everything else. If Abram would but set his face toward the land, leaving the old things behind, God would do the rest.

What is the land? This we must recognize, for we are going to meet this land of Canaan throughout the Word of God. Perhaps you have heard it described as heaven. It is not heaven, except in the sense that heaven begins here on earth. It is not some state that we must wait to enter until we die. It is intended that we should, like Abram, enter it at the beginning of our Christian life, and live in it all our days. What is the land then?

It is simply life in Christ. It is what the New Testament calls *the fullness of the Spirit*. It is life controlled by the Spirit of God, reflecting the glory of Christ. We enter it by conversion, but we do not experience the fullness of its blessing until we learn, like Abram, to adjust ourselves to its peculiar demands. But it is the land of promise, the land of fulfillment, the land of God's blessing and power. The whole of the Bible is written for no other purpose than to bring the people of God into the land of God. This is where he called Abram to go.

At this point in the record there comes a little interlude which we must consider. We are told that Abram obeyed God and started out for the land, but he stopped along the way. The record of those wasted years at Haran is found in Genesis 11:31- 32.

> *Terah took Abram his son and Lot the son of Haran, his grandson, and Sarai his daughter-in-law, his son Abram's wife, and they went forth together from Ur of the Chaldees to go into the land of Canaan; but when they came to Haran, they settled there. The days of Terah were two hundred and five years; and Terah died in Haran.*

As far as we know from the record, Terah never heard the call that Abram heard. He left Ur, not in order to enter the land of Canaan, but simply to get

away from Ur! The call of Abram made him recognize
that Ur did not offer a life satisfying to the heart, and
when he saw that his son was determined to leave,
Terah said, "I'll go along." As the father and head of
the family, he went out; but only as far as the land of
Haran, half-way to Canaan. How powerfully this pictures those who attempt to gain the promise of the
gospel by leaving Ur (the world and its ways), but
who never enter Canaan!

There are thousands today who have left Ur and
come to Haran. But they have settled there, and there
they will die. The word Haran means "parched" and
it is indeed a parched and barren place to live. Many,
like Terah, have left the world and its ways. They
may have joined a church. They have got religion.
They live moral lives, they sing the songs of Zion and
they go through the outward motions of faith. But
they will never go farther than Haran. They are dying
there; they are religious, but not born again. What a
parched experience that is!

But Abram was there, too! He left Ur by faith and
was on his way to Canaan . . . but he wasted many
years in Haran. While he was there, there was no dis-
cernible difference between him and his father. He
was not yet ready to fully obey God, for he had not
left his father's house—dependence on his own resources—as God had commanded. As a result, he
wasted seventy-five of his one hundred and seventy-
five years. Finally Terah died, and when the old man
was gone, Abram was free to go on into the land of
Canaan.

I hope you follow the typical significance of this. If
we depend upon our own resources to be acceptable
to God, he must take them all away. He will let us go
on for a long time so that we may learn the weakness
and folly of such a life. But finally he will take them

away. When he does, we think it is a dreary day for us—but it is really the greatest day of our lives. Only then are we free to enter the land, where we may learn to depend upon God alone.

Now as Abram comes into the land, we have a revealing description of life there:

> *So Abram went, as the LORD had told him; and Lot went with him. Abram was seventy-five years old when he departed from Haran. And Abram took Sarai his wife, and Lot his brother's son, and all their possessions which they had gathered, and the persons that they had gotten in Haran; and they set forth to go to the land of Canaan. When they had come to the land of Canaan, Abram passed through the land to the place at Shechem, to the oak of Moreh. At that time the Canaanites were in the land. Then the LORD appeared to Abram, and said, "To your descendants I will give this land." So he built there an altar to the LORD, who had appeared to him. Thence he removed to the mountain on the east of Bethel, and pitched his tent, with Bethel on the west and Ai on the east; and there he built an altar to the LORD and called on the name of the LORD. And Abram journeyed on, still going toward the Negeb (Genesis 12:4-9).*

This is more than just a record of what happened to Abram when he first entered the land. It is an accurate picture of the conditions of a Spirit-filled life. The first thing we are told is that Abram passed through the land to the place at Shechem, to the oak of Moreh. These names are most revealing. Shechem means "shoulder," and the shoulder is to the Hebrew a symbol of strength. We think of the shoulder of a

mountain in the same way. The name Moreh means
"instruction." When we combine these two words,
we get our first glimpse of what it is like in the land.
Only as we are taught the Word of God by the Spirit
of God do we find strength to live.

> *Like newborn babes, long for the pure spiritual*
> *milk, that by it you may grow up to salvation*
> *(1 Peter 2:2).*

The second picture we have here is that life in the
land is to be a life of constant conflict. We read, "At
that time the Canaanites were in the land." These
Canaanites were the pagan tribes which afflicted Israel all through its history. When Israel came back
into the land after its stay in Egypt, God ordered the
extermination of these tribes; but Israel failed to carry
it through. Therefore, these people hounded,
bothered and afflicted Israel the whole of its history.
They are thus a good picture of those evils we live
with and continually wrestle against. They are
named for us in the New Testament in many places:
lust, envy, jealousy, impatience, intemperance, ir-
ritability, touchiness, etc. They are our daily
enemies—these outbursts of self which make for continual conflict.

Third, it is also a life of continual cleansing, for we
next read, "So he built there an altar to the LORD."
We think of an altar as a symbol of worship, which it
is, but that is not the essence of its meaning. An altar
is first a place of cleansing which provides the basis
for worship. The reason for a daily altar is the urgent
need for cleansing in the pilgrim life. Every pilgrim
needs the cleansing of blood, the cross of Christ, to
which he can come and judge self as it exhibits itself
in his life. So many Christians seem to feel they need
the cross only at the beginning of their Christian life;

but that is not true. We need it every day, for it is the
word of the cross which is the power of God in daily
life. This is why Paul cries, "I die every day" (1 Corinthians 15:31). This life of the Spirit must be one
of continual cleansing by the cross of Christ.

Fourth, this is a life of unending choice. Abram
pitched his tent between Bethel and Ai. Bethel
means "the house of God," Ai means "ruin." This is
just where we must live the Christian life, ever looking either to the things of God or to the ruin of the
flesh. We can choose to go to Bethel or to Ai, to
Christ or self—it can never be both. I am either pleasing myself, or pleasing him. I am either at Bethel,
the house of God, or at Ai, the place of ruin. I must
continually choose.

The last characteristic is represented by the tent.
What did Abram do when he got to the land? He
journeyed on! He never stopped for long. He lived in
a tent because he was a pilgrim. He could never settle
down; he could only sojourn for awhile. All through
the New Testament the Christian pilgrim is exhorted
to walk in the Spirit. Walk, walk, walk! When you
have learned a lesson from God, that is not the end.
That is just another step. Tomorrow there is another
step to be taken, and another the day after that, and
another the day following. How the flesh resents this!
We are always delighted when the Spirit of God
drives us to the place where we achieve some victory,
overcome some habit, take some needed step. And
then we want to settle down there. We say to the
Lord, "You go on for awhile and leave me here. I want
to enjoy this for a bit." But he will not let us stop.
Life in the land is a life of continual progress, a never-
ending journey.

Everyone is living in one of three places—Ur,
Haran, or Canaan. *Where do you live?* What a question

to search the heart! Ur is the land of death and darkness, the land into which we were born. Haran is the
half-way house where we gain the outward appearance of being religious but where there is no inward
reality. Canaan is the land of power and blessing, the
place of the Spirit's fullness. Have you entered the
land?

As we continue our study of the life of Abraham,
let us determine to wholeheartedly follow the command of God, for only then may we rise up to go into
the land of fullness of blessing in Christ. Let us remember that every word God says is true and that
every promise will be fulfilled. And let us hear the
voice of God saying to us, "Arise, get up, go out from
your country, your kindred, and your father's house,
into that land which I will show you!" *That* is the
road to success. There is no other.

This is the
way - walk ye in it.
There is a way that seems R~

2
THE HIGH COST OF LETTING DOWN

(Genesis 12:10-13:4)

It is refreshing to meet a real pilgrim in the midst of our secular, security-loving age with its continual emphasis upon comfort, convenience, and compromise. We can identify pilgrims by two invariable symbols: a tent and an altar. Not that such people actually live in tents; but their whole outlook is transitory, like those who live from campsite to campsite. They hold material things loosely and are conscious of the fleeting, ephemeral values of what the world thinks important. There is a discontent with what the earth offers and a hunger for something more. This is the tent. The second characteristic is the altar, the place of self-judgment where true worship is found. It means having a low opinion of one's own abilities and a high opinion of God's. It is an awareness of the constant need of cleansing and a dependence upon a power greater than self.

The story of Abraham is the story of such a pilgrim. It takes us back several thousand years to the other side of the cross; but the spiritual history of this man is as up-to-date as if he were born in the twentieth century. With his tent and his altar, Abram sojourned in the land of Canaan. He had no permanent home, but moved about from place to place. The land of Canaan, as we have already seen, is a picture of the Spirit- filled life. It is not a place of special privilege, as many think. It is not a place which invites only the great and the favored few. The land of Canaan is where God expects every Christian to dwell every day of his life, twenty-four hours a day!

Though Abram is now in the land, he has not yet learned the conditions of life in the land. He stands in the same place as any new Christian who is now "in the Spirit" but has not yet learned to "walk in the Spirit." And as so often happens at this stage of the Christian life (as we pick up the story of Abram in Genesis 12), we find it is the story of the failure of faith. What new Christian has not discovered what it is to lose his sense of joy and his awareness of the presence of Christ? We shall find the reasons for this perplexing experience traced here in three movements: the famine in Canaan, the folly of Egypt, and the fullness of God in the land.

The account begins in chapter 12, verse 10:

Now there was a famine in the land. So Abram went down to Egypt to sojourn there, for the famine was severe in the land.

The land of Canaan was much like parts of California—a wonderful land with a magnificent climate, but dependent upon the limited rainfall for water. There are times when there is no rain and the land suffers a drought, becoming parched and dry, and the grass withers. For those whose livelihood depends on pasturing flocks this is a dangerous time. Abram was a man with flocks and herds, and when the rains failed these were severely threatened. He saw his immediate source of sustenance endangered, and it must have seemed increasingly impossible to remain where he was. As the scarcity of food grew, he felt driven to leave, even though God had called him to be there.

There is not a word here about asking God's permission to go down to Egypt. Abram took counsel, not from God, but from his fears alone. To use a contemporary expression, he "pushed the panic button," and down to Egypt he went. It was fear that drove him. Now if the land is a symbol for us of the life of fellowship with a living Christ, then a famine in the land is any circumstance that threatens our dependence upon him. It is any circumstance that makes faith difficult. Have you ever experienced such a famine? Have you been living in the full joy of fellowship with Christ when the strength of God is yours, and suddenly some circumstance beyond your control makes it hard to maintain that fellowship?

It may be a new boss who turns out to be an ogre; it may be neighbors who throw their garbage over the back fence; or a tiger of a mother-in-law who comes to live with you. It is always some difficult circumstance of life that makes it hard to maintain fellowship with Christ. Perhaps it is hard and demanding labor that leaves you little time for cultivating the spirit. It may be a bitter disappointment that crushes you, making your heart ache and leaving you with little strength for prayer and fellowship. It may be the continual oppression of depressing surroundings which are hard to rise above. It may be misunderstood motives—you meant to do good but someone took it wrong and you have been cut to the quick. In short, it is any temptation that seems more than you can bear and which threatens to cut off your very strength, your fellowship with Christ.

When this occurs, we are tempted to flee rather than to stick it out. We do not enjoy trials like this, and we try to get away—physically, if we can. We move to another neighborhood, change jobs, take a trip, or go home to mother. If we cannot flee physically, we try to run away mentally. We escape the unpleasant reality by a flight into unreality. There is so much of this today—some retreat into a mental Egypt where life seems more pleasant.

Once, perhaps, it was a simple problem of daydreaming. But now we can have it done for us electronically through the television set. "Dr. Parker's Fourth Wife" is brought to us in picture as well as sound. Many live in that realm of fantasy all day long. Or maybe you begin to haunt movie theaters for distraction from your worries. Or you find a perpetual din from the radio keeps you from disturbing thoughts or from quietly, thoughtfully facing life as it really is. Perhaps the retreat you choose is a constant round of social life or the overloaded weekend. Far too many Christians demonstrate that the spirit is willing, but the flesh is ready for the weekend! Some retreat to alcohol or to overeating, forgetting that an overhang is perhaps as bad as a hangover. Whenever we attempt to satisfy the spirit with the resources of the world, we have gone down to Egypt.

There is a vast difference between this escape and

the occasional need for recreation and rest which God himself recognizes: "Come away by yourselves to a lonely place and rest a while" (Mark 6:31). Nor is Abram's flight into Egypt a warning to us that we should have nothing to do with worldly people. We are expected to live our lives in the midst of the world and its ways. But going down to Egypt means adopting the attitudes, the expectations, and resources of the world. It is trying to slake the thirst of the spirit at a dry cistern.

Abram's experience here is given to teach us the unutterable folly of Egypt:

> When he was about to enter Egypt, he said to Sarai his wife, "I know that you are a woman beautiful to behold; and when the Egyptians see you, they will say, 'This is his wife'; then they will kill me, but they will let you live. Say you are my sister, that it may go well with me because of you, and that my life may be spared on your account." When Abram entered Egypt the Egyptians saw that the woman was very beautiful. And when the princes of Pharaoh saw her, they praised her to Pharaoh. And the woman was taken into Pharaoh's house. And for her sake he dealt well with Abram; and he had sheep, oxen, he-asses, menservants, maidservants, she-asses, and camels. But the LORD afflicted Pharaoh and his house with great plagues because of Sarai, Abram's wife. So Pharaoh called Abram, and said, "What is this you have done to me? Why did you not tell me that she was your wife? Why did you say, 'She is my sister,' so that I took her for my wife? Now then, here is your wife, take her, and be gone." And Pharaoh gave men orders concerning him; and they set him on the way, with his wife and all that he had (Genesis 12:11- 20).

Now let us see what happens in Egypt. First of all, the pressure is off! Abram found in Egypt the release he was seeking. There was a famine in Canaan; he felt its pressure; he ran away from it and immediately found the pressure relieved. There was plenty to eat in Egypt. And it is far more comfortable and relaxing to live in a house in Egypt than in a tent in Canaan. But this is not the whole story.

What else happened in Egypt? It is plain that when Abram lost his faith he also lost his courage! Even before he got into Egypt he grew afraid and descended to cowardice and falsehood. He told "a little white lie" (that is what we would call it today). He said to his wife, "Look, dear, I know these Egyptians. I read about them in the library in Ur. They are all wolves, and you are a beautiful woman. I know what will happen when we get down there. They will want to take you, and if they know you are my wife, they will kill me. Let's play it smart with a little strategy. You tell them you are my sister."

This was not wholly a lie. Sarai was Abram's half-sister. She was the daughter of a woman who married Abram's father after Abram was born. So this was a half-truth. But a half-truth is also a half-lie, and a lie in any proportion is intended to deceive. The nearer it is to the truth, the more perfectly deceitful it is. Abram's intent was clearly to deceive. Doubtless he justified it on the grounds that it was needed to protect his beautiful wife. Perhaps this is the most startling thing about this story. Sarai was sixty-five years old at the time, yet so remarkable is her beauty that Abram is afraid he may lose her, and when the Egyptians see her they immediately take tales of her beauty to Pharaoh. Abram feels cast upon his own resources to defend her, and his only recourse is to lie.

This is the first result of moving out of Canaan and

out of fellowship with Christ. Out of the land, away from the tent and the altar, old self comes to the fore and assumes control. The immediate result is hypocrisy and deceit. Have you found that to be true? The minute you begin to move away from the control of God, your old self, with its defensive mechanism against being hurt, comes to the surface and you stoop to falsehood, hypocrisy, and deceit.

The outcome of this lie was that Sarai was put into a place of real danger. The king claimed her for his harem, and it was the lie Abram told that opened the door. The danger he thought existed had no power to harm her until he made it possible by his lie! This is the second folly of Egypt—our loved ones suffer because of our cowardice and deceit. Abram was trying to protect himself, but in protecting himself he exposed Sarai to ignominy and danger.

This is the trouble with Egypt. It is true the pressure we fear is relieved there, but when we try to live on the resources of the world we lose our own strength and endanger those who look to us for help. Not only was Sarai endangered, but Lot also. Abram's nephew, Lot, went down to Egypt with him. Later on, when the allurements and enticements of the cities of Sodom and Gomorrah cast their spell over Lot, we are told that he saw the land as though it were the plain of Egypt. The lust for comfort and worldly glory that was born during this stay in Egypt almost destroyed him then. Remember that when you flee to Egypt, your loved ones are being hurt as well as you.

The third factor about Egypt is that Abram was made very rich. You say, "What's wrong with that? This is not an evil but a blessing." Perhaps, but it was Jesus himself who used the phrase, "the deceitfulness of riches," referring to one of the things which could choke the Word in a person (Mark 4:19). In Egypt, Abram was given sheep, oxen, he-asses, men-servants, maidservants, she-asses, and camels. This is the wealth of the oriental world. But when he comes back into the land, the first thing we hear of is strife between his herdsmen and Lot's herdsmen over the riches they got in Egypt. Furthermore, we are told he was given maidservants. One of them was named Hagar, with whom Abram later conceived the child, Ishmael, the father of the Arab nations (who ever since have been a thorn in the side of Israel). The price of living in Egypt is a fearsome one indeed.

But this is not all. Abram became a curse to the worldlings with whom he lived. "The LORD afflicted Pharaoh and his house with great plagues because of Sarai, Abram's wife." He was called to be a blessing, but when he got into Egypt, he became a curse instead! A Christian out of fellowship with Christ is of no help to the lost people around him. Instead, he is a hindrance. His life of hypocrisy and weakness is a stumbling block and a plague upon the hearts of those who watch him. In God's name, if you are not walking in the fullness of the Spirit, do not attempt to witness to anyone about Christ. You will become a curse to them if you do.

Finally, Egypt is a place of rebuke and humiliation. What a scene this is! Here is Abram, the man of God, standing before this pagan king who has better morals than he has, being publicly rebuked for his folly.

Years ago, when I was a young Christian living in Denver, Colorado, I took on the job of soliciting advertisements for a small church paper. The pastor felt that some businesses which dealt with the church would be willing to put an ad in our little paper. I was to call them on the telephone and solicit the business. One of those I called was the manager of a prominent restaurant nearby. I opened the conversation by telling her I was calling for Mr. Hewitt, the pastor of the church, as he had given me permission to do. Evidently she misunderstood and thought that I was Mr. Hewitt. Throughout the conversation she addressed me as Mr. Hewitt. It took me by surprise at first, and I did not correct her at the time. She placed an ad, and the next month I called her again to renew it. It had worked so well to be mistaken for Mr. Hewitt that I thought I would tell her it was he calling again. I got another ad.

The third month I tried it again. But this time her voice grew cold and distant as she said, "I don't know who you are, but you are not Mr. Hewitt, for as I sit here in my office I can see Mr. Hewitt and his wife eating lunch. I don't know what kind of church you run, but if this is the means you have of getting business then don't bother with me anymore." And she hung up the phone. I can still feel the shame and humiliation of that moment as though it were yesterday. What a terrible place of rebuke and folly is Egypt!

But now God terminates the painful lesson of Egypt in Abram's life. At the deepest moment of his agony, crushed with humiliation and sick at heart, Abram comes out of Egypt, tarred and feathered and riding on a rail, back into the land of Canaan. We read, "Pharaoh gave men orders concerning him, and they set him on the way, with his wife and all that he had." "Good riddance, Abram, we're through with you!" What a sad price to pay for the release from pressure that Egypt affords.

Once back in the land, he finds again the fullness of supply that he could have had all along!

*So Abram went up from Egypt, he and his wife,
and all that he had, and Lot with him, into the
Negeb. Now Abram was very rich in cattle, in
silver, and in gold. And he journeyed on from the
Negeb as far as Bethel, to the place where his tent
had been at the beginning, between Bethel and Ai,
to the place where he had made an altar at the first;
and there Abram called on the name of the* LORD
(Genesis 13:1-4).

As soon as Abram is back in the land, there is the
tent and the altar again. There is no tent or altar in
Egypt. That is, there is no pilgrim character, no
place of worship or cleansing, no fellowship in
Egypt. But even back in the land, Abram must come
back to the place where he had made an altar at the
first; and there Abram calls upon the name of the
LORD. In other words, time spent in Egypt is wasted!
There was no growth in grace in that land. He had to
come right back to where he was when he went down
to Egypt. He had material gain to show for the time
in Egypt, but nothing but barrenness and weakness
spiritually.

Have you discovered how true this is? When you
forsake the pathway of faith, when you refuse to walk
in fellowship with God, when you depend upon the
resources of the world to satisfy the empty hunger of
the heart—these are wasted years! They may literally
be *years*. I know Christians who have lived almost all
their Christian lives in Egypt, and all they have to
show for it is a barren, wasted, empty, dreary, boring
existence.

When Abram at last returned, what did he find?
There is no mention of famine when he returns, but I
think the famine is still going on. Remember,

Abram was *driven* out of Egypt. He was not yet ready to leave it of his own choice, and this would indicate the famine was still raging in Canaan. Also, the quarrel which developed with Lot's herdsmen over the pasture land suggests there was still a severe shortage of feed. But though the famine still continues, Abram is no longer troubled about it. Why not? Because when he reached the land, the first thing he did was to call on the name of the LORD! This is what he should have done and could have done when the famine first struck.

The name of the LORD stands for all the resources of God. When we cash a check we are calling on the name of the man who signed the check. When Abram calls on the name of the LORD he is discovering the resources of God. He discovers that God is able to meet his needs despite the famine, the trial, or the circumstances. Just as Paul proclaims, "And my God will supply every need of yours according to his riches in glory in Christ Jesus" (Philippians 4:19).

In the closing days of Hudson Taylor's life the Boxer Rebellion broke out in China. Every day reports were coming to missionary headquarters of the death of national pastors, or the persecution and imprisonment of missionaries. It seemed that all that Hudson Taylor had given his life to was crumbling before his eyes. One black day, after some particularly distressing news had come, Hudson Taylor's associates wondered if it would be too much for the old man. He spent the morning in his house alone, and when they came to see him in the afternoon, they trembled at what they might find. But as they approached the house, they heard him singing to himself:

Jesus, I am resting, resting,
In the joy of what Thou art;
I am finding out the greatness,
Of thy loving heart.
Thou hast bade me gaze upon Thee,
And thy beauty fills my soul,
For by thy transforming power,
Thou hast made me whole.

Are you in a time of testing and trial that makes it difficult to hang onto God? Do not think for a moment you will find what you need by running down to Egypt. You will find a kind of relief, but the price of Egypt is terrible.

For the soul that says, "It's all right, Lord, I'm looking only to you to see me through," there awaits a sure and full supply of God—that inner strengthening of the heart that makes it possible to meet whatever trial may come in the joyfulness and glory of faith.

3
LETTING GOD
CHOOSE

(Genesis 13:5-18)

Someone has pointed out that life seems to be arranged backwards. We are called upon to make our most important choices at a time when we have the least amount of experience to guide us. It is because of this that we so frequently hear expressions of regret like, "If only I had known . . . ", "If I had it to do over again . . . ", etc. It is this very quality of life which reveals our inability to handle life by ourselves. It is a wise person, indeed, who learns this lesson early and gives heed to the biblical admonition, "Trust in the LORD with all your heart, and do not rely on your own insight. In all your ways acknowledge him, and he will make straight your paths" (Proverbs 3:5-6).

After the temporary failure of faith which took Abram from Canaan into Egypt, we find him once again in the land, with his tent and his altar, enjoying the fullness of divine supply. As we saw earlier, however, life in the land is one of continual conflict; we must go from victory to victory. Furthermore, it is a life of unending choice. We are now given an illuminating account of what happens when strife and trouble break out in the Christian life. Who has not stood at this place?

> *And Lot, who went with Abram, also had flocks and herds and tents, so that the land could not support both of them dwelling together; for their possessions were so great they they could not dwell together, and there was strife between the herdsmen of Abram's cattle and the herdsmen of Lot's cattle. At that time the Canaanites and the Perizzites dwelt in the land. Then Abram said to Lot, "Let there be no strife between you and me, and between your herdsmen and my herdsmen; for we are kinsmen. Is not the whole land before you? Separate yourself from me. If you take the left hand, then I will go to the right; or or if you take the right hand, then I will go to the left" (Genesis 13:5-9).*

We have been reading of Lot all through the story of Abram. He was Abram's nephew, and he came with him out of the land of Ur. The whole story of this man is told in one brief phrase in verse 5: ". . . Lot, who went with Abram." That sums up Lot's whole life. He went with Abram! Wherever Abram was, Lot was. When Abram stopped, Lot stopped. "With Abram"—that is all that can be said of him.

Many commentators seem to think Abram was wrong to take Lot with him out of the land of Ur. There is no doubt Lot was a continual weight around his neck. But Scripture never implies that it was wrong to bring Lot along. Lot evidently responded when God spoke to Abram and called him to go out into a land which would be shown him. Lot wanted to go along, and Abram, wishing to help him, agreed. The trouble is not with Abram but with Lot.

Lot pictures those Christians who depend upon others for faith and inspiration to act. There are many Lots around. They never seem to learn to walk alone with God, but lean on another's faith for strength. As long as they have a strong church to lean on, or a close friend who is a faithful Christian, or they can listen to a gospel radio station all day long, or they have a Christian magazine coming regularly, then all goes well. But where the prop is weak, they are weak also. When Abram's faith failed, Lot's faith failed. Lot leans on Abram all the way. He is a second-hand Christian. Although his own faith is genuine (and the New Testament makes it clear that Lot was a righteous man), nevertheless he depends wholly upon Abram to make his service effective.

This works well as long as the pressure is on. As long as things are a bit rough, Lot will stay with Abram; for he senses his need for the strength of the man of faith. Lot feels his weakness to act upon his own faith. There are many like this. As long as things are a bit difficult, they lean hard upon their Abram, whoever or whatever it may be. But there is one kind of test this type of Christian cannot stand—the test of prosperity, when all goes well. Material prosperity, especially, will always show up the Lots in our midst.

So we read here that when their possessions became so great they could no longer dwell together, strife came between them. Today we would call this a conflict of interests. There are many parallels in modern life. Here are two partners in business, both of them Christians. For the stronger of the two, the man of faith, this business exists for only one purpose: to benefit the work of God. He knows that God expects him to take his normal living from it, but that is not why he is working. His real reason for working is that he may use the strength and wisdom God gives him to invest and make money to advance the work of God.

At first, the other partner goes along with him and agrees that his goal is a worthy basis for the business. But prosperity comes! They make a little money, the second man raises his standard of living and gets his eyes on the material things of life. He becomes more concerned about increasing the business and making a big thing of it than about anything else. When that happens, there is only one thing to do. As with Lot and Abram, there comes a time for a dividing of the ways; and it is the man of faith who takes the initiative. Lot would have let this thing fester until it broke out into some serious conflict, but Abram says, "There is only one thing to do. We must separate now before there is any further difficulty."

> *Then Abram said to Lot, "Let there be no strife between you and me, and between your herdsmen and my herdsmen; for we are kinsmen. Is not the whole land before you? Separate yourself from me. If you take the left hand, then I will go to the right; or if you take the right hand, then I will go to the left" (Genesis 13:8,9).*

Note the reasons Abram gives for this separation. Every word here is important. In the last part of verse 7 we are told, "At that time the Canaanites and the Perizzites dwelt in the land." Why is this mentioned here? Is it not a warning to us that whenever strife looms between Christians, the enemies of the Lord are ready to take full advantage of it? These Canaanites and Perizzites, dwelling in the land, represent the evils of the flesh that lurk in every Christian heart: jealousy, envy, resentment, bitterness, malice, etc. They are always ready to spring into action if there is any dissension or grievance between Christians. Abram acted before they awakened, for he knew they were in the land. Everyone's heart harbors something that, if allowed to fester, will come to the fore, and he will be possessed by the spirit of jealousy, resentment, or bitterness. Abram acted before this could happen.

The second reason is found in his words, "Let there be no strife, for we are kinsmen," that is, "brethren." We are brethren! That means we are tied together in the same bundle of life, and if I hurt you I am hurting myself. If you hurt me, you are hurting yourself. Brethren cannot have strife without injuring one another. Whenever strife develops between members of the Body of Christ, it always has this result. It is a case of cutting off your nose to spite your face. If you hurt your brother, you are surely hurting yourself.

Abram, in his God-given wisdom, said, "Let us not have any of this. We are brethren, so do not let this become an issue between us. Let us calmly settle the matter now before it breaks out in open conflict." Then Abram did a magnificent, God-honoring thing; he gave up his own rights without a murmur. He was the older man of the two and the acknowledged

leader, Lot's superior in every way. Yet he said to
him, "Lot, you take the first choice, I give up my
right to it. If you want to go this way, I'll go that
way." How evident it is that the tent and the altar
have already done a work of grace in this man's heart!

I once heard Dr. H. A. Ironside tell of an experience in his early life when his mother took him to a
meeting where two Christian men almost came to
blows over a disagreement. One man finally stood
and pounded the desk and shouted, "I don't care what
you do, but I will have my rights!" At that, an old,
partially deaf brother, who had been sitting nearby,
leaned forward, cupped his ear in his hand and said,
"Eh? What's that? What did you say, brother? Your
rights is it? Is that what you want? Ah, brother, if
you had your rights you'd be in hell! The Lord Jesus
didn't come to get his rights—he came to get his
wrongs, and he got them." And with that the bel-
ligerent fellow flushed and sat down saying, "You're
right, you're right, settle it any way you like." Soon
there was perfect agreement. It was this same spirit
that moved Abram to give Lot the first choice.

Now we learn what happens when Lot chooses:

> *And Lot lifted up his eyes, and saw that the Jor-
> dan valley was well watered everywhere like the
> garden of the LORD, like the land of Egypt, in the
> direction of Zoar; this was before the LORD de-
> stroyed Sodom and Gomorrah. So Lot chose for
> himself all the Jordan valley, and Lot journeyed
> east; thus they separated from each other. Abram
> dwelt in the land of Canaan, while Lot dwelt
> among the cities of the valley and moved his tent as
> far as Sodom. Now the men of Sodom were wicked,
> great sinners against the LORD (Genesis 13:10-
> 13).*

inspiration

Evidently Lot and Abram went out on a promontory overlooking the valley and Lot lifted up his eyes. What did he see? It is obvious he only looked in one direction. He had been out looking around before! Without hesitation now, he looked to the east and saw the well-watered plain below like the garden of the Lord in the midst of the desert. He saw the Jordan River cutting through its great gorge, the deepest point on the face of the earth. On either side of the Jordan the lush green grass was growing, and the variety of palm trees made the whole place a veritable garden. He was greatly attracted to it; it was a modern real estate developer's dream!

Then he saw the cities of the plain. They were like Egypt! Lot remembered Egypt as a place where one could get rich quick, with its vast commercial enterprises and its blind materialism. This is what Lot saw as he looked across the valley.

But the passage suggests there were some things Lot did not see. Although the Jordan Valley was there before his eyes, he did not see the significance of its name. The word "Jordan" means death. The river descended out of the living waters of Galilee and dropped far below sea level into the Dead Sea, from which there is no outlet. It was grand to look upon; but spiritually it meant the place of death. This Lot failed to see.

Then it is specifically pointed out that the men of Sodom were wicked—great sinners before the Lord. Lot saw the profitability of these cities, but he did not see their moral corruption. The name of Sodom today is linked to a particularly revolting form of sin. Though the life of the city was morally rotten, it was hidden beneath an attractive prosperity. We have our Sodoms today. Moral corruption has permeated our

social life and is something we must consider as we
face the choices of life. This Lot failed to do.

We are told yet another thing that Lot missed:
"this was before the LORD destroyed Sodom and
Gomorrah." Here is a mention of the judgment that
was to come. Lot saw the prosperity and the beauty,
but he did not see this was a place marked out for
judgment; it was all to be swept away forever.

Now, it is true that neither Lot nor Abram could
foresee the death, the rottenness, the judgment that
life in Sodom would bring. But the whole point of
the story lies right here. Lot, presuming to run his
own life, "chose for himself." Deceived by what he
saw, he stumbled blindly into heartache and judgment. Abram, on the other hand, was content to let
God choose for him, though it looked second-best.
And long before the true nature of Sodom became apparent to Lot, Abram saw it in its true light.

When will we learn that the inner nature of
things—things as they really are—is only revealed to
the man with the tent and the altar? It is only as we
become pilgrims, remembering that we do not have
our final dwelling place here on this earth, that the
Word of God unfolds before us and we see something
of the judgment, the moral corruption, the deadly
character of what otherwise looks so attractive.

So we read, "Lot chose for himself." What a telling
phrase that is! As he looked out, Self said, "Ah, this
will advance you, this will make you prosperous, this
will give you status and position." So he chose *for
himself* and pitched his tent toward Sodom. Every
time he moved his tent, he moved it ever nearer
Sodom. We shall see more of what this meant in a
later chapter.

But now, what happened to old Abram? How did

it go with the man who was willing to let God make the choices for him?

> *The LORD said to Abram, after Lot had separated from him, "Lift up your eyes, and look from the place where you are, northward and southward and eastward and westward; for all the land which you see I will give to you and to your descendants for ever. I will make your descendants as the dust of the earth; so that if one can count the dust of the earth, your descendants also can be counted. Arise, walk through the length and the breadth of the land, for I will give it to you." So Abram moved his tent, and came and dwelt by the oaks of Mamre, which are at Hebron; and there he built an altar to the LORD (Genesis 13:14-18).* Abe's Lot

Lot had lifted up his eyes and chosen for himself; now God says to the man of faith, living in his tent on the hillside, "Abram, lift up your eyes." Where? Everywhere—to the north, the south, the east (the portion Lot chose), and the west. All the land is his! This land is consistently a symbol of the fullness of life in the Spirit of God; the life of joy, power, love, and glory; the life of refreshing ministry to others. Surely this is what Paul longs for us when he prays, "That you may have power to comprehend with all the saints what is the breadth and length and height and depth, and to know the love of Christ which surpasses knowledge, that you may be filled with all the fullness of God" (Ephesians 3:18,19). This is all yours, if you are willing to let God make the choices of life for you.

Lot will never know this! Nor will we, if we make our choices on the basis of what we see, relating to the materialistic, commercial standards of those about us. But if, like Abram, we are content to have what God gives us in life, all the fullness of Christ will be ours. Paul says in 1 Corinthians 3:21-23: "For all things are yours, whether Paul or Apollos or Cephas or the world or life or death or the present or the future, all are yours; and you are Christ's; and Christ is God's."

Then God said to Abram, "Not only do I give this land to you, but I will fill the land with your descendants." That is, "I will make you fruitful beyond belief. I will make your life one of such blessing that after you are gone there will be those who will stand up and say, 'I received my spiritual life through that man; there came to me strength for my journey through him; he has been a great blessing to me.'"

Then he said to Abram, "Arise, walk through the length and breadth of the land, for I will give it to you." The land is all that Christ will be to us through the eternal ages to come. But God is saying to us, "Don't wait for it. You don't have to wait until you die to enjoy this. You can have it now, if you will possess it. Walk through the land. Set your feet upon it. Possess it—now!"

If we, seeing Abram walking up and down the land, had said to the Canaanites and Perizzites, "Do you know who this man is? This is the owner of all this land!" they would have looked at us with pity, laughed, and continued on their way. But it was true! Wherever Abram wanted to move in that land, God opened the door. The whole land was his. He could go where he wanted. He could live where he chose. The Canaanites and the Perizzites had to move out when Abram came in. Thus also the Spirit of God declares to us in Romans 6:14: "For sin will have no dominion over you, since you are not under law but under grace." Whenever you want to be free from the weakness, and ruin, and power of sin, you can! The land lies open before you. Possess it!

So we read, "Abram moved his tent and came down to the the oaks of Mamre." Mamre means "fatness," the place where the soul is made fat with the fullness of supply. And there at Hebron, which means "fellowship," he built an altar to the Lord. In the place of fatness and fellowship, Abram confessed again by the building of an altar that he was nothing but a fallible human being, without strength in himself, needing the constant cleansing of God. It is a wonderful picture, isn't it?

Everyone dwells in a world exactly like that of Abram and Lot, a world in which material values constantly clamor for us to make a choice. We have only so much time to invest, so much life to spend, and we are pressured to grab the best for ourselves while we can. We can say with Lot, "I want what the world can offer me now, I want the cities of the plain." Or we may wait with Abram, content with our tent and altar, enjoying the blessings of the land by faith now, and waiting for God's fulfillment of all his promises in the wonderful age yet to come. The Christian who is content to let God make his choices finds it easy to fulfill the New Testament word: "give thanks in all circumstances, for this is the will of God in Christ Jesus for you" (1 Thessalonians 5:18).

4
WHEN YOU NEED
A FRIEND

(Genesis 14:1-16)

Many think the Christian life is prosaic, dull, uneventful. It is anything but that! If it appears that way, it is almost certainly a life out of focus with true spirituality; in other words, a carnal Christian life.

We have seen already that whenever Abram is found with a tent and an altar in the land of Canaan, he is a wonderful picture of a Christian living in the power and joy of his pilgrim life—in this world but not of it, daily judging self by the cleansing of the cross. Lot, on the other hand, pictures the carnal Christian, flesh-governed, living for self. He has forsaken the place of fellowship with Christ. Lot left Abram on the hillside and moved down toward

Sodom and Gomorrah, the cities of the plain. He was
drawn by the allurements of the world and began to
live for himself and for the pleasures of life. He pictures a Christian who is born again, but enmeshed in
the enticements of the materialistic, commercialized
world around.

But now, suddenly, Abram's quiet and pleasant
life is shattered. *Life in the Spirit is like that.* We are
never permitted to rest beside the still waters very
long, nor would we want to, for life there soon grows
dull and uninteresting. In Genesis 14 we are introduced to the first war ever recorded in Scripture. It is
a stirring account, vividly contrasting the blustering
armies of earth with the quiet, overcoming power of
faith. We get our first glimpse of these earthly armies
in the first three verses.

> *In the days of Amraphel king of Shinar, Arioch
> king of Ellasar, Chedorlaomer king of Elam, and
> Tidal king of Goiim, these kings made war with
> Bera king of Sodom, Birsha king of Gomorrah,
> Shinab king of Admah, Shemeber king of
> Zeboiim, and the king of Bela (that is, Zoar).
> And all these joined forces in the Valley of Siddim
> (that is, the Salt Sea) (Genesis 14:1-3).*

The spade of the archaeologist has amply verified
the existence of the kings named here. Long before
the rise of the Babylonian Empire, these kings made
a military foray into the land of Canaan, perhaps to
defend their trade routes with Egypt or to subdue the
warlike tribes of the area. The account here could
have been taken from the daily newspaper of Sodom;
the city recognized the threat to its welfare and liberties, and was much alarmed.

As the account progresses, we learn that Chedorlaomer is the chief of the invading kings. Histori-

cally, he is identified as the Elamite dictator from the land east of Persia, now known as West Pakistan. He came with his satellite kings against a confederacy of five monarchs from the cities of the plain. His coming in this way represents the world's power to harass and enslave Christians. But more than one type is required to portray the whole aspect of the world's enmity. Sodom, for instance, pictures the world in its lust for sensual pleasures. In contrast to this, the invasion from the east portrays the world in its naked power to enslave and tyrannize and take away the physical liberties of man.

These forces are often found opposed in history. Our own beloved nation of America is already enslaved to the forces of materialism, greed, and sex. These forces dominate our national life. But it is also threatened by an outside force, communism, which ruthlessly seeks to destroy our physical liberties and enslave the nation. Here are two differing forces, both arising out of the fallen nature of man. One desires material gain, economic advancement, luxury, ease, and sensual pleasure. The other is sheer, naked tyranny, threatening our very physical existence.

This is exactly what confronted the cities of the plain, and Lot especially, as he now dwelt in Sodom. Lot is already enmeshed in the blind commercialism of Sodom, but has kept himself free from the sexual degradation of the place. Now he is threatened by circumstances that would deprive him of basic liberties.

How does this relate to us today? It might be some form of legalism, or perhaps some vicious habit such as alcoholism or sexual abuse. It might even be a sickness that renders one a bedridden invalid—although all sickness is certainly not of this sort. Whatever may be the problem, it is something outward that threatens physical or spiritual liberty. Here is Lot, a

carnal Christian, caught between the jaws of a vise—
the materialism of Sodom and the tyranny of Chedorlaomer.

Verses 5-7 reveal the apparent invincibility of this
enemy:

> *In the fourteenth year Chedorlaomer and the kings
> who were with him came and subdued the Rephaim
> in Astheroth-karnaim, the Zuzim in Ham, the
> Emim in Shaveh-kiriathaim, and the Horites in
> Mount Seir as far as El-paran on the border of the
> wilderness; then they turned back and came to En-
> mishpat (that is, Kadesh), and subdued all the
> country of the Amalekites, and also the Amorites
> who dwelt in Hazazon- tamar.*

Rephaim and Zuzim were families of giants. It is
from this group, later in Israel's history, that Goliath
came, whom David decapitated with his own sword.
These were men eight to ten feet tall, a mighty race
who were greatly feared by those around them. Yet
the invading kings swept away even these giants.

The territory mentioned here is quite extensive,
covering from the north and west of the Sea of
Galilee, down the Jordan Valley, all the way south to
the Red Sea. Here, then, was an enemy, seemingly
invincible, relentless, unstoppable, striking fear into
every heart as he relentlessly crushed all opposition.

At this point we have the first mention of Lot. If it
were not for him, we would know nothing at all of
these events; the Bible never reports any human history except as it relates to the peoples of God.

> *Then the king of Sodom, the king of Gomorrah,
> the king of Admah, the king of Zeboiim, and the
> king of Bela (that is, Zoar) went out, and they
> joined battle in the Valley of Siddim with Chedor-*

laomer king of Elam, Tidal king of Goiim, Am-
raphel king of Shinar, and Arioch king of El-
lasar, four kings against five. Now the valley of
Siddim was full of bitumen pits; and as the kings
of Sodom and Gomorrah fled, some fell into them,
and the rest fled to the mountain. So the enemy took
all the goods of Sodom and Gomorrah, and all
their provisions, and went their way; they also took
Lot, the son of Abram's brother, who dwelt in
Sodom, and his goods, and departed (Genesis
14:8-12).

It is specifically called to our attention that in the valley of the Dead Sea there were many tar or bitumen pits, filled with natural asphalt. If you have visited the La Brea Tar Pits in Los Angeles, you will know just what is described here. These open pits of asphalt would be covered over by the desert sand as the wind blew across them and they would appear like the surrounding ground. But anyone venturing into such a pit would be held by the tar and his body would be imprisoned for centuries. The bones of dinosaurs and other beasts have been found in the La Brea pits, having been encased in tar for many centuries. Evidently the five kings of the confederacy felt that this area would be the best place for battle, as the pits would be a natural defense. But instead they became a trap. As the tide of battle turned against them, they fled to the mountains in headlong haste. Many of them, falling into the pits of tar, were destroyed. In the ensuing capture of Sodom, Lot, his family, and all his goods were carried away by the invading army.

Perhaps you have fallen into just such a circumstance. You have tried to fight back, but nothing seems to avail. The very defenses upon which you rely become threats against you. You can choose capture

or falling into the slime pits, one or the other. And
perhaps, as Lot, you have found yourself captured
against your will by some evil habit or power that enslaves you.

Then notice what happens! The Holy Spirit shifts
the scene to Abram up on the mountainside, so that
we might see the overcoming power of faith. All hope
for Lot now lies in Abram's hand:

> *Then one who had escaped came, and told Abram
> the Hebrew, who was living by the oaks of Mamre
> the Amorite, brother of Eshcol and of Aner; these
> were allies of Abram (verse 13).*

A messenger comes to Abram, perhaps sent by
Lot. At the last moment before his capture, he may
have hurriedly sent this man out to slip through the
lines and find his way to Abram. It is likely that he
barely escaped from the clutches of the enemy with
his life. He finds Abram in Hebron, the place of fellowship. With him are three men who are his allies.
Mamre, as we have noted before, means *fatness or
richness.* Eshcol means a *group* or *bunch*, and Aner
means an *exile, one who withdraws himself.* Taking
these three names together, spiritually speaking, I
see a prayer meeting here! Here is a group of people,
living in the richness of fellowship with Christ, who
have withdrawn themselves from the ordinary demands of life for a specific purpose. This is exactly
what our Lord bids us do in Matthew 6:6a: "But
when you pray, go into your room and shut the door
and pray to your Father." Abram the Hebrew is lead-
ing the meeting. Since this is the only place in Scripture where Abram is called a Hebrew, it must have
some special significance. The word Hebrew means
passenger, or *pilgrim.* The Spirit of God would high-
light for us the character of the ones to whom Lot

looks for rescue. They are led by the man who holds lightly the things of earth, the man of the pilgrim life.

To this band on the hillside comes the message that Lot is in trouble. When Peter, in the New Testament account, was put in prison, we are told that the church prayed for him without ceasing. As a result the doors of that prison were flung back, the iron gates were opened, the shackles fell off and Peter was led out by an angel. When a child of God through ignorance or selfish folly has fallen into something that enslaves and grips and holds him, the only answer is the believing prayer of the people of God. That is what we have here.

Now let's see how victory is achieved:

> *When Abram heard that his kinsman had been taken captive, he led forth his trained men, born in his house, three hundred and eighteen of them, and went in pursuit as far as Dan. And he divided his forces against them by night, he and his servants, and routed them and pursued them to Hobah, north of Damascus (Genesis 14:14,15).*

Here is the key to victory—three hundred and eighteen men, trained for warfare! Now, this was not his entire battle force. There were other men belonging to Abram's allies, but this is the hard core of trained, disciplined men he relied upon to lead his little army into battle. He had only three hundred and eighteen, but that was all he needed! It might have seemed a pitiful handful beside the vast armies of those four kings who had come out of the ancient east, plundering everything before them as they came. But if we will learn the lesson taught here and all through Scripture, we need never be discouraged by overwhelming numbers again. The lesson is simply this: God's victories are never won by force of numbers! Never! "Not by might, nor by power, but by my Spirit, says the LORD of Hosts" (Zechariah 4:6b).

If three hundred and eighteen people were to gather to pray today, that would be a red letter day indeed. And if those three hundred and eighteen people knew how to pray, were trained in the warfare of prayer, they would shake the powers of evil around the world! Three hundred and eighteen would put to rout all the vast armies of the enemy.

Our world is threatened by the tremendous power of communism, and many of our brothers and sisters around the world are grievously threatened by fear if they stand firm in their faith. I fully believe God is showing us that the whole secret to the defeat of this terrible enemy will lie in a relative handful of people, who here and there will faithfully get together and recognize that victory does not lie in the might of weapons, of nuclear missiles, or diplomacy, but in men and women of faith who are pilgrims and strangers here in this world, and who will regularly separate themselves from the demands of life and seek the mind and face of God. Then the forces of tyranny will be routed in many places, and men and women who are now enslaved by the pitiless, ruthless chains of atheistic communism will be set free.

Note the careful strategy Abram employed. We are told he divided his forces by night. The march of Abram and his tiny band is one of the most remarkable forced marches in history. They traveled the whole length of the Jordan River, coming upon the enemy considerably north of the Sea of Galilee. As was the custom with armies of that day, when the pagan invaders had withdrawn to a place they considered safe, they made camp for several days and indulged in a time of carousing and reveling in celebration of their victory. It was at such a time and place that Abram and his allies found them, and during the night, they divided their forces and surrounded the drunken camp. Abram sent one part of his army one way and one the other, one group perhaps with spears and the other with swords for close combat. At a signal, they sprang upon the surprised host and there was a general rout and a great victory.

This division of Abram's forces into a two-pronged attack suggests the Christian's weapons in spiritual warfare. In Ephesians 6, we are reminded that we possess two effective weapons—the Word and prayer.

> *And take the sword of the Spirit, which is the*
> *Word of God. Pray at all times in the Spirit, with*
> *all prayer and supplication . . . for all the saints*
> *(Ephesians 6:17,18).*

Many a "Lot" has been delivered from the slavery which bound him by the helpful counsel of the Word of God given through some fellow-believer, and the prayers of the men and women of God who have supported him. Thus Abram divided his forces, and using a twofold approach, he set the enemy to flight.

Notice yet a third incident. Abram pursued them as far as Hobah, north of Damascus. Hobah means "hidden," and therefore signifies a complete victory, even to the point of the enemy hiding himself to escape. Abram never let up. He kept on till the forces against him were demoralized. He pressed his advantage to the utmost. He did not quit fighting, he did not stop praying at the first little break, but pressed on through until he won a great and tremendous victory. In verse 16, we see the extent of the victory Abram won:

*Then he brought back all the goods, and also
brought back his kinsman Lot with his goods, and
the women and the people.*

Now in all this, the Holy Spirit would drive one
thing home to our hearts. We do not lead our Christian lives in seclusion— we are members one of
another, and in circumstances of this nature, one
Christian can often be the means of deliverance to a
weaker brother or sister. There was nothing Abram
could do to deliver Lot from Sodom. Sodom represented an inward choice in the heart of this man. Lot
chose to live in the materialistic, sensualized atmosphere of Sodom. If a child of God chooses to be
materialistic, sensual, commercial, greedy for things
of the world . . . not much can be done for him. Only
Lot could take himself out of Sodom. But from this
circumstance that threatened Lot's very life and liberty, Abram's resources were ample.

James 5:16b tells us, "The prayer of a righteous
man has great power in its effects." There is an excellent Chinese translation of that verse: "The earnest,
hot-hearted prayer of a righteous man releases great
power." That is certainly the case in this incident.
"The prayer of faith," we are told in the same chapter
of James, verse 15, "will save the sick man and the
Lord will raise him up." Many have been puzzled by
this verse, but if we read the context, we see that the
affliction is one that has come because a child of God
has become involved in deliberate sin. Such a one is
to call the elders of the church together and confess
his faults. Then the prayer of faith will save the sick,
the Lord shall raise him up again, and he will be delivered from the thing that has held him captive.

It is wonderful, this power of prayer for someone
else. The history of the church is replete with such

[handwritten margin note: Lot didnt ask 4 help there]

[handwritten margin note: maybe Aby was praying O wd jolt Lot - that's ok - cuz Abe was rdy to help]

deliverances through faithful prayer. Some time ago, a wise and experienced missionary leader, speaking to a group of us about prayer, talked about overwhelming sin that so grips the heart as to enslave the life and frustrate all activity for God. He gave some very wise words of advice.

"Perhaps some younger Christian," he said, "may find himself in such a circumstance, and the thing he is doing is so shameful that he cannot bring himself to confess it publicly; then let him seek out some older man of God, someone he can trust, and lay the whole matter out before him and ask him to pray concerning this."

It is wise counsel, indeed. When Lot could not possibly help himself, Abram, separated in heart from the Sodom-like attitudes that rendered Lot so powerless, was able to lay hold of God and effect a great and mighty deliverance.

5
THE PERIL
OF VICTORY

(Genesis 14:17-24)

Following Abram's great victory over the invading kings from the east, the fourteenth chapter of Genesis relates a curious incident with a strange and mysterious king named Melchizedek. The book of Hebrews makes so much of Abram's encounter with Melchizedek that our curiosity is awakened and we are stimulated to find out more about this man of mystery. We may be sure that the deliberate interjection of this account at this point in Abram's life is designed by the Spirit of God to help us in our own lives of faith.

Abram is now on his way back to Sodom with all the goods of the city and much of the population,

including Lot and his family. It is a time of victory
for Abram, and therefore a time of peculiar peril. In
our spiritual life, the enemy loves best to strike when
we are relaxed and off-guard after some spiritual victory or period of great usefulness. His approach then
is never open or frontal, but subtle and insidious,
taking full advantage of our relaxed defenses. Let us
note how Abram is suddenly confronted with a subtle
temptation on his way back to Sodom, how by a
strange interlude deliverance comes to him, and observe his sensible attitude toward others in this incident.

> *After his return from the defeat of Chedorlaomer
> and the kings who were with him, the king of
> Sodom went out to meet him at the valley of Shaveh
> (that is, the King's Valley) (Genesis 14:17).*

Our special attention is directed to the place where
the king of Sodom met Abram on his way back from
the battlefield. It was a valley right outside the little
village of Salem. In later Israelite history, Salem was
transformed into Jerusalem, the capital of all Israel.
The valley outside the city, even then known as the
"King's Valley," was none other than the Valley of
the Kidron, the little brook that ran down along the
eastern side of Jerusalem, separating the mount of
Olives from the city. It was into this valley that our
Lord went with his disciples on the night he was be-
trayed, crossing over to go up the slopes of the Mount
of Olives to Gethsemane's garden. In this strategic
and historic spot, the king of Sodom met Abram.
Skipping down to verses 21-23, we read:

> *And the king of Sodom said to Abram, "Give me
> the persons, but take the goods for yourself." But
> Abram said to the king of Sodom, "I have sworn to*

*the LORD God most High, maker of heaven and
earth, that I would not take a thread or a sandal-
thong or anything that is yours, lest you should
say, "I have made Abram rich."*

Here is the subtle temptation which suddenly
came upon Abram. He was met by the king of
Sodom, who had somehow escaped capture and was
in the city when news came of the triumphant return
of Abram with the spoils of war.

On the surface, the king's offer seems a perfectly
justifiable reward. Abram had fought his great battle
not on behalf of the king of Sodom, but for the sake
of Lot and his family. Nevertheless, his victory
greatly benefited that whole wicked city. That is why
the king was there to meet him. A special welcoming
committee had been appointed, headed by the king
himself, to confer upon Abram the usual reward for a
conquering hero. The king simply asked for the return of the residents of the city; the goods and riches
he gratefully offered to Abram. The wealth of Sodom
was all to be Abram's!

Now notice the subtlety of this temptation. It appeared so right and proper! Abram could well have
said, "This is certainly only what I deserve, and after
all, it is the custom to do this. Everyone does it!
There are no strings attached. I can take the wealth
and go my way back to my tent and altar and never
go near Sodom again." Who of us, standing in
Abram's shoes, would not have thought like this?

But it was exactly in the apparent freedom of the
gift that the peril lay. To a man of Abram's character,
it is impossible to accept this kind of a gift without
feeling an obligation to the giver. If he had been required to sign some kind of contract, he would have
found it easy to say no; but to accept this gift without

strings would be to make it exceedingly difficult to say no to anything later on. From that day on the king of Sodom could say, "Abram is indebted to me. If I ever need any military help, I know where I can get it. My man is up there on the hillside." The gift was an insidious threat to the independence of the man who took orders from no one but God. If Abram yielded, he would never be wholly God's man again.

Note the timing of the temptation: it came when he might well be off-guard, enjoying the popularity of the hour. He had earned a few moments of relaxation after the strain of battle, and at this quiet moment in his life the subtle offer came. Have you experienced something like this? I have seen young Christian college students surrounded throughout the school year by subtle and perilous dangers to their faith and fellowship with Jesus Christ, and who maintain proper safeguards, keeping alert, aware of the peril that confronts them. But when they come home on vacation, they let down their guard and there comes some sudden and appalling failure. Satan has chosen that moment to attack.

There is no doubt that the pressure on Abram to accept this gift was very great. It was an expression of gratitude on the part of the king, and I am sure that Abram felt the king would be hurt if he rejected this sincere offer. I have found that many Christians, myself included, have been trapped by the fear of offending someone if we say no. We are troubled about what they will think, and so often very little troubled about what God will think. We fail to realize if we cannot say no now, how can we ever say no after the offer has been accepted and we are indebted to some degree? The easiest time to say no is now!

This is what the apostle Paul meant when he wrote, "All things are lawful for me, but I will not be

enslaved by anything" (1 Corinthians 6:12b). That
is, the only one I wish to serve is Christ. The only
power to which I will yield my life is his. Anything
else that threatens to control me or limit me I reject!
It may be lawful, it may even be in good standing all
around; but if it makes any demand upon me that is
not his demand, I do not want it! This is what Abram
so beautifully demonstrates here.

He replies to the king of Sodom, "I have sworn to
the LORD God Most High, maker of heaven and
earth, that I would not take a thread or a sandal-
thong or anything that is yours, lest you should say,
'I have made Abram rich.'" Note the positiveness of
that decision. He says, I will take nothing; not a
thread, not even a shoestring! I do not care what you
offer me, I want nothing. No thing. Period. That
settles it! More emphatic language is simply not possible. *didn't run the King down*

And note the solemnity of what he says. This is
tremendously important to Abram. It is not some
mere passing whim. He says, "I have sworn to the
LORD my God." This touches the deepest thing in
his life. He takes a solemn vow that he will not touch
anything of Sodom's. And how perfectly frank he is:
"lest you should say, 'I have made Abram rich.'" In
other words he is saying, "I want you to know why I
have done this. I can serve only one king at a time,
and I want you to understand that I am not concerned
for my own enrichment, least of all through you. If it
doesn't come to me through my God, to whom I have
committed my life, and from whom I have determined to accept whatever he offers, then I don't want
it."

It is a bold and positive declaration, is it not?
What a clear-cut victory! The subtle trap of the
enemy has been uncovered and the danger is safely

past. The Lone Ranger escapes unscathed again! Ah,
but why? This is what we are interested in. How is it
Abram saw through this subtle thing so clearly, and
so stoutly resisted those almost overpowering pressures? Now let me put it to you bluntly: If you were
in Abram's shoes that day, knowing your own heart,
would you have offended the king by rejecting his
grateful offer? I am sure my own devious heart would
have viewed it as an added bonus from God, as a result of my great faithfulness to him in battle, and I
would have accepted Sodom's gift. Abram did not!
Yet he was a man like me, of like passions and heart.
How, then, could he pass this test so easily? The answer lies in this strange interlude with Melchizedek
which we have passed over till now, verses 18-20:

> *And Melchizedek king of Salem brought out bread*
> *and wine; he was priest of God Most High. And*
> *he blessed him and said, "Blessed be Abram by*
> *God Most High, maker of heaven and earth; and*
> *blessed be God Most High, who has delivered your*
> *enemies into your hand!" And Abram gave him a*
> *tenth of everything.*

Before the king of Sodom met Abram with his wily
offer, Abram had already met with another king, the
mysterious Melchizedek. This king steps suddenly
out of the shadows, ministers to Abram, and just as
suddenly disappears from the pages of Scripture. We
never hear another word about him until we come to
Psalm 110, where David declares that the Messiah to
come is made a priest forever after the order of Melchizedek. Then another thousand years roll by, and
in the book of Hebrews we have another extended
reference to this strange individual. Who was Melchizedek? The guesses range from Shem, the son of
Noah (who according to some chronologists could

still have been alive at this time), to an appearance of
the preincarnate Christ in human form.

All we are definitely told is that he is the king of
Salem (which afterwards became Jerusalem) and that
he is the priest of the Most High God (Hebrew: *El
Elyon*). His own name means "king of righteousness."
He appears suddenly in the Scriptural record without
any mention of father or mother—in a book, remember, replete with genealogies—no birth date,
and no subsequent account of his death. These omis-
sions from the record are seized upon by the writer of
Hebrews to indicate that since we have no record of
his genealogy, this man is a type of the eternal priesthood of our Lord Jesus Christ who literally has no beginning or end of days, but who ever lives to make
intercession for all those who come unto God by him.
Thus, the Melchizedek priesthood is a ministry of
help to those who face a time of trouble.

Here, then, is a man who is evidently a Gentile
king. The original knowledge of God as the maker
and possessor of the heavens and the earth, passed
along by Adam to his descendants, has evidently
come down to Melchizedek unchanged. He is a worshiper of the true God, and a priest to that true God.
In this sublime presentation of Scripture the record
shows him in such a way that he becomes a type of
our Lord Jesus who is our heavenly Melchizedek,
ready to minister to us in our needs. His specific
ministry is to reveal *El Elyon*, the Most High God,
the One who owns everything in heaven and on earth.
He is the one perfectly adequate to meet any human
need. This is what Paul declares in Philippians 4:19:
"And my God will supply every need of yours according to his riches in glory in Christ Jesus."

Now we can see why God led Abram back to his
home by way of the King's Valley. The king of

Sodom is coming to meet him, but Abram knows nothing of his approach nor of the subtle offer with which he plans to put Abram in his debt. Had he known of it, he may have seen nothing wrong with it, for Abram is not different from you and me. The peril is too subtle to detect; it looks too innocent and attractive. So God sent Melchizedek to meet him!

His first ministry to Abram was to remind him of the character of the God he served. Perhaps he warned Abram of the subtle trap awaiting him in the offer of Sodom's wealth, and then he may have said, "Abram, your God is the possessor of heaven and earth. He made it all. He owns it. He holds all its wealth in his hands. There is nothing that he cannot give you. This is the God to whom you belong."

And then we are told he served him bread and wine. We need no interpreter for this. These are the symbols of love. They speak eloquently of strength and joy flowing out from the passion of self-giving love. All this is recorded in the Old Testament, yet as we read it we can see a beautiful picture of the need of our own lives. There is nothing with such power to motivate the Christian heart as when a group of believers partake of these symbols of the suffering of our blessed Lord. He gave himself in the fullness of his life, poured out all that he was. And as we feast by the Spirit upon the symbols of his life, that life strengthens the inner man, lends sinew to the resolve of the soul, and makes us able to meet all that comes our way. This is the only power sufficient to make us reject the world's offer and maintain our independence as servants of Christ. The love of Christ constrains us!

In the intimacy of this fellowship, under the ministry of Melchizedek, Abram worships his God. The record says he gave him a tenth of everything—

that is, he gave him tithes of all he had. The tithe is
not a debt paid to God; it rather symbolizes that
everything belongs to him. The antitype in the New
Testament is not that we continue to give a tenth, as
under the law (nor as in this case in patriarchal days),
but to recognize that all we are and have is to be given
to God in worship. In 2 Corinthians 8:5, Paul writes
of the Macedonian Christians: "But first, they gave
themselves to the Lord and to us." The whole of our
life is to be focused on the one aim of serving God.

Here in the King's Valley, where centuries later a
greater Melchizedek would sweat in bloody agony in
a garden, Abram enjoyed by faith the high priestly
ministry of Christ. His heart overflowed with the
love of Christ. Refreshed and strengthened in spirit,
he saw that God alone could satisfy his heart. There
was no other place where he could find the deep-
seated satisfaction that makes the rivers of living
water begin to flow. Here he swore to the Lord his
God he would not touch a single thing that Sodom
could offer him, and in the strength of this encounter, he rose up and went out to meet the fair and
innocent- appearing trap. Now he was ready for it!

Have you ever found yourself trapped by some subtle appeal that looked innocent enough and seemed
to be the popular thing to do? Too late you realized
its true nature, when the damage had already been
done; and all you could say was, "I didn't realize . . .
I never dreamed . . . I meant right."

You may remember an account of an unfortunate
young man who perjured himself some years ago in
connection with a TV quiz program. Everyone wondered at his apparently endless knowledge of difficult
subjects. When he was finally exposed as having been
given the right answers beforehand, he told the court
that it had all looked so innocent. He justified his

deceit to himself on the basis that he was advancing
the cause of intellectualism and education. He believed that as people saw him give these almost impossible answers, they themselves would be stimulated to learn more. He knew some would regard it as
cheating; but it was justifiable as advancing a good
cause. Then, at last, he realized what he had done,
and he confessed it. "I was deceived, deluded," he
said. "I couldn't see the way it really looked until it
was too late."

North?
Pointer?

This happens to many of us, doesn't it? Life is full
of subtleties like this—little decisions, little problems, small incidents that seem so innocent on the
surface. We find it easy to rationalize and justify our
choices. Why is it we fail? It is because we do not go
to our Melchizedek! We give him no opportunity to
minister to us and open our eyes. We do not come to
the throne of grace, as we are bidden, to find grace to
help in time of need.

We are like poor, troubled Martha, stewing over
her pots and pans in the kitchen until, out of patience, she comes storming into the parlor to blame
the Lord Jesus for all her problems! Luke gives us the
story in his Gospel (Luke 10:38-42). Martha meant
to make the Lord welcome in her home, she intended
to fix him a delicious meal. Yet she ends up so frustrated and bewildered that she insults him and ac-
cuses him of causing the whole mess. In contrast, the
Lord suggests that Martha needs what Mary had
found. What was Mary doing? She was sitting at
Jesus' feet, letting him open her eyes to truth. She
was letting him possess her heart; and as she did, she
found life falling into place. The right things were
being emphasized. She saw things in their proper
perspective and focus.

Abram would never have passed by this subtle trap
unscathed had Melchizedek not met him. In the intimacy of that fellowship, he saw what he would not
otherwise have seen: that the values on which the
world sets great store are but baubles compared to the
glory of fellowship with a living God, maker of
heaven and earth. When the king of Sodom came,
Abram could say, "Take your little toys and run back
to Sodom. I want none of it. I want no man to say
that he has made Abram rich. If anyone makes
Abram rich, it will be God." What a victory!

One more incident is brought before us in this
story. It is the very sensible attitude Abram displayed
toward the others who were involved with him in this
affair. He says to the king of Sodom, "I will take
nothing but what the young men have eaten, and the
share of the men who went with me; let Aner, Eshcol,
and Mamre take their share" (Genesis 14:24).

Abram, do you mean to say it is right for these
young men to have what is wrong for you to take? Is
it possible to have a double standard of right—one
for you and another for them? What a lesson there is
here for us! These young men had not yet come to the
stage of Christian living and maturity that Abram
had achieved. There is no Melchizedek for them—or
if there was, they did not enter into the same depth of
comprehension that Abram did. Abram is content to
let God deal with them directly in these borderline
areas. He is not going to force others to walk in the
light of his conscience.

Somehow, Abram has learned the truth of Romans
14, that we are not to judge our brother in these matters: "Let everyone be fully convinced in his own
mind" (verse 5b). I have had Christians tell me that
God had spoken to their hearts and told them it was

wrong for them to drink coffee, and they have tried to persuade me to stop, too. But I am still waiting for word from the Lord on this! I recall hearing of a dear old Nazarene evangelist called Uncle Bud Robinson. He spoke with a slight lisp and was well-known and well-loved by Christians throughout the west. Among certain groups borderline issues are frequently raised, and whenever anyone would say to Uncle Bud, "How can a man drink coffee and still be a Christian?" he would say, "Juth bring me a cup and I'll thow you."

It is a great lesson to learn that there are areas of our Christian life where we must walk alone before our God, and cannot force our views on others. So Abram says, in effect, "Let the young men have their share. It is not right for me to take anything, but they are not standing in my place. Let them have their share."

Life lies ahead of us with all its possibilities of peril and danger, both spiritual and physical. How we need to go on in the strength of the Lord our God, maker of heaven and earth! Nothing that the world offers can fully meet our hearts' need. All that will really satisfy comes from him alone. We are in this world. We are expected to live in it. We are expected to use the world, but not to abuse it. We must not love it, nor demand anything from it. Like Abram, we must lift our hand and say, "I have sworn to the LORD my God, I will not touch anything that you have to offer."

How gracious is our God to send us that blessed, heavenly Melchizedek to strengthen us in times of peril, and to enlighten our hearts! How clearly we see the need for fellowship with him! How dare we face the perplexities and complexities of this subtle world apart from daily fellowship in the King's Valley with him? What easy prey we are to the snares of Satan without this. Let us, then, be forever grateful that we can be delivered daily through the great and loving power of the Lord Jesus.

6
FAITH
CONQUERING
FEAR

(Genesis 15:1-6)

The opening paragraph of Genesis 15 strikingly illustrates what is commonly called in Bible study, "the law of first occurrence." This principle says that the first time a word or phrase is used in the Bible, it is used in such a way as to fix its basic meaning throughout Scripture. Four such phrases appear in this passage for the first time in the Bible, though they are repeated many, many times afterward. See if you can recognize them:

> *After these things the word of the LORD came to Abram in a vision, "Fear not, Abram, I am your shield; your reward shall be very great." But Abram said, "O LORD God, what wilt thou give*

me, for I continue childless, and the heir of my
house is Eliezer of Damascus?" And Abram said,
"Behold, thou hast given me no offspring; and a
slave born in my house will be my heir." And be-
hold, the word of the LORD came to him, "This
man shall not be your heir; your own son shall be
your heir." And he brought him outside and said,
"Look toward heaven, and number the stars, if you
are able to number them." Then he said to him,
"So shall your descendants be." And he believed the
LORD; and he reckoned it to him as righteousness
(Genesis 15:1-6).

Did you catch the first one, in the very first line,
"the word of the LORD came"? The recurrence of this
phrase many times afterward in Scripture emphasizes
the God-breathed character of the Bible. The word of
the Lord came to many men, just as it came to
Abram; they wrote as they were borne along by the
Holy Spirit and then sat down and studied these writ-
ings to learn what God had said (1 Peter 1:10-12).

The second phrase is the word that came to
Abram, "Fear not!" How often this is God's word to
man throughout this book! The third phrase is, "I am
your shield." In a thousand wonderful variations, we
find this thought repeated frequently: God is our
refuge and our strength . . . God is a tower of refuge
. . . God is an overshadowing rock . . . Blessed is he
that hides under the shadow of the Almighty. This is
the first mention of this character of God in Scripture. And then there is that familiar word in the last
verse: "And he believed the LORD; and it was
reckoned to him for righteousness." The fires of the
Reformation were lit from that ringing phrase!

The heart of this passage does not lie in its great
phrases, but in its connection with the preceding

events of Abram's life. God appears to Abram in a vision, but when he comes his first words are, "Fear not!" This reveals what is going on in Abram's heart. He was having a sleepless night and the trouble was that he was afraid! Coming, as this incident does, after Abram's return from his battle with the four eastern kings and his encounter with the king of Sodom, we can see why he is so fearful. He is afraid of this man, Chedorlaomer, the great king whom he had conquered. Abram had publicly humiliated him by overthrowing his vast army with but a handful of men. Dictators do not take this kind of treatment lightly!

We can easily understand Abram's fear as he faced a possible return of Chedorlaomer. No doubt he said to himself, "What have I gotten myself into? I am almost sorry that I won this battle; for when he comes back, what am I going to do? I won't be able to catch him off guard another time." So fear fills his heart.

Perhaps also there was fear because he had turned down the king of Sodom's offer of a fortune. He did it, of course, in the strength of the fellowship he had enjoyed with Melchizedek. With his heart aflame with the love and grace of God, Abram had said to this king, "I want nothing of all that you have. I don't want you saying that you made Abram rich." So the king went back to Sodom with all his riches, and now Abram is back in his tent, acting very human. Compared to the wealth and luxury of Sodom, that tent must have looked inexpressibly shabby. The wind howled around it; the sand sifted through its cracks. So doubt begins to rise in Abram's heart—did he do the right thing? And doubt is a form of fear!

If all this sounds familiar, take comfort from the fact that it's a natural reaction. All the great saints of

God suffer from it. There may have been a time in your life when you took a stand for God in the strength of his grace, supplied to you at that moment . . . and yet later you wondered if you did the right thing. That is only what you might expect. Abram's heart quaked with this clutching fear: what would happen when Chedorlaomer came back? And by throwing away the wealth of Sodom, had he made a wise decision? Or had he played the fool?

Still further, deep down in his heart, was a lurking loneliness, a gnawing fear that he had somehow misunderstood the promises of God. It had been ten years since God had said to him, "Abram, I am going to give you a son. Your descendants will be as numerous as the dust of the earth, and you shall become the father of many nations." Ten years of waiting had passed. "Hope deferred makes the heart sick, " says the proverb. The sickness was beginning to creep into his soul.

We may gather from his words that he was beginning to wonder if perhaps the Lord had meant he would give him an heir, but it would not necessarily be his own son. Perhaps it would be a foster son, even a servant such as Eliezer whom he bought in Damascus. On this sleepless night, I think the old man was trying to adjust to this possible solution; but he could not quiet that inner sense of loneliness and disappointment. So he tossed and turned in a mounting spiral of fear, doubt, and loneliness.

I am sure if this had happened to us, we would have taken a couple of aspirin or tranquilizers and gone back to sleep. If Abraham had, of course, he would have missed the whole marvelous revelation of God's love! There are times when Christians are perfectly justified in using tranquilizers, but there are also many times when to do so is to miss God's purpose in trial. To run to the drug cabinet whenever anything goes wrong, to be unwilling to allow any unrest or bit of tension, to insist that life must maintain a steady, even keel at all costs and under every circumstance, is to thwart and miss the very purpose for which God sends difficulties into our lives. He only desires to create an atmosphere where he can be glorified.

But as Abram tossed on his bed at night in his tent, he became aware of a Presence with him. In his heart he hears that mysterious word of the Lord. Sometimes God spoke audibly to these Old Testament men; sometimes it was in the heart, with a quiet, deep conviction that God was speaking. Every Christian who has ever walked in fellowship with Jesus for very long knows what I mean. We are not told how God spoke to Abram, but in the midst of his fear and doubt and loneliness there comes a sense of relief. The word of the Lord comes and says, "Fear not, Abram. I am thy shield and thy exceeding great reward. I am the sufficient answer to all your fear!"

Of course God is the answer! If God be for us, who can be against us? If God is our shield, whom should we fear? I love that verse in Hebrews, "He has said, 'I will never fail you nor forsake you.' Hence we can confidently say, 'The Lord is my helper, I will not be afraid; what can man do to me?'" (Hebrews 13:5,6). "I am thy shield." That is what comforted Abram's heart there in the darkness. It was all he needed to settle his worries about the return of Chedorlaomer and the loss of his fortune in Sodom.

Have you learned yet to count on the invisible protection of God? Can you stand before danger as our Lord did before Pilate, and say, as he did in John 19:11: "You would have no power over me unless it had been given you from above"? Oh, the sense of the

invisible shield of God! As someone has well put it,
the Christian is immortal until his work is done.
Nothing can touch him nor hurt him except it come
by permission of God, who is a living shield around
him. We would lose most of our fears if we realized
this. Each believer is as safe as one of those TV western stars in the midst of a gun fight! You know that
the star of the program is not going to die. It may
look as though he is in mortal danger, but he never
really is. Not, at least, until the sponsor is ready to
drop the show!

How many times it seems we live charmed lives.
A number of years ago, my wife and I were driving
across New Mexico. We were in wild and lonely
country, driving along about sixty miles an hour. For
some time I had heard a continuous grinding noise.
On my car that was not unusual, but I finally decided
this was a little out of the ordinary so I stopped to
investigate. I noticed the hub of the right front wheel
was hot and smoking. I jacked up the car, and when
the weight was lifted the front wheel fell off and
rolled into the ditch. We had heard that grinding
noise for some ten miles, and to this day I am certain
that the wheel stayed on throughout that distance
simply because of the protection of God.

This is what God is saying to Abram: "I am your
shield, Abram, a practical defense against any force
that would destroy you. Fear not. Nothing shall
touch you unless I permit it. Do not fear—I AM!"
Have you noticed how many times in the New Testament our Lord Jesus calms his disciples with these
words, "Fear not"? The ground of his reassurance is
always that he is with them. When the storm
threatens to overwhelm the little boat; when the cold
fist of fear clutches their hearts as they sense the
shadow of the cross on their path; when Peter goes

weeping bitterly out into the night; it is then his words ring in their ears—"Fear not, let not your heart be troubled" (see John 14:1). Why? "Believe in God, believe also in me!"

But God is more than a shield. He says also to Abram, "I am your exceeding great reward." (The Authorized Version is to be preferred here.) God is our dearest treasure, the only genuinely satisfying joy we will ever know.

One evening my wife and I were invited to a neighborhood party. We welcomed the opportunity to become better acquainted with our neighbors. When we arrived we discovered that it was a cocktail party, and it had been in progress for an hour or so. We were greeted warmly (not to say hilariously) at the door and soon were being introduced to many of our new neighbors. Most were in a cheerful mood, to all appearances having the time of their lives. But I could soon see it was highly artificial. Though there was an outward attempt at happiness and enjoyment, there was also written on every face a haunting emptiness, an expression of meaninglessness and futility. We were both struck by this. They were doggedly determined to have a good time; they insisted they were doing so, despite the hunger and desperation evident in every word and glance. We felt so sorry for those dear people. We said afterwards we would not trade one moment of the riches of grace in Christ for a whole lifetime of that kind of enjoyment. Sensing the presence of God is a far richer joy than anything else the human heart can find.

This is what Abram experienced when God said to him, "I am thy shield and thy exceeding great reward." We never again read of Abram worrying about Chedorlaomer or the loss of Sodom's wealth. All these pressures from without were fully met by

a father's fear
being childless!
No Legacy?!
I failed G!
(godliness infertile)

the sense of God's presence with him, there in the
dark.

Ah, but that other request that is in his heart! That
vacuum of loneliness within. Could God fill that?
And there comes blurting out of the heart of Abram
these words, "O LORD God, what will thou give me,
for I continue childless, and the heir of my house is
this Eliezer of Damascus." In the intimacy of that
moment, he simply poured out what was in his heart
into the ear of his Almighty Friend. And God said,
"Get up and come outside with me." And he led him
out into the soft oriental night and together they
looked up into the stars, wheeling in their silent
courses above. Abram must have felt something of
the awe of spirit which comes to those who see the
blazing heavens at night and sense the insignificance
of man. There God said to him, "Abram, I am going
to give you a son. Your servant will not be your heir.
I will give you a son and that son shall have sons, and
they in turn will beget sons, and you will have a great
host of descendants. Now look up at the stars and tell
me how many there are, for if you can number the
stars, you will be able to number your descendants,
for just so many will there be."

This is a great promise, out of the greatness of
God's heart. It must surely have reassured and en-
couraged Abram. Each night to come, until the
promise was fulfilled, he could look up into the starlit
heavens and remind himself of the promise God had
made.

There is something of great interest here. The last
time God had spoken to Abram about the birth of a
son, he had promised he would make Abram's descendants like the dust of the earth. But now the
promise is that they shall be like the stars of the
heaven in multitude. Many Bible scholars have sup-

posed this implies that Abram would have two lines
of descendants: an earthly seed and a heavenly one.
The earthly seed would be the nation Israel, along
with the Ishmaelite (Arabian) nations. But there
would also be a heavenly or spiritual seed. That
"Seed," we are told in the book of Galatians, was
Christ and all those who through faith in him would
be called the sons of God.

As we look back now from our twentieth-century
vantage point, we can see how God has fulfilled these
promises to the letter. There is an earthly seed, but
there is also a heavenly one, a great uncounted host of
spiritual descendants of Abraham, like the stars of
the heaven in multitude. Paul says in Galatians 3:7,
"So you see that it is men of faith who are the sons of
Abraham."

Now the last statement in this interesting paragraph in Genesis 15 comes before us. It concerns
Abram's faith. "And he believed the LORD; and he
reckoned it to him as righteousness." Paul refers to
this mighty act of faith in Romans 4. He reminds us
that Abraham believed God before he was circumcised—that is, before he had any continual guarantee
that God would do this thing. The account of
Abram's circumcision comes a couple of chapters
later. Paul infers from this that acceptance before
God has nothing to do with circumcision (as the Jews
were insisting). Paul says that when Abram heard
God say, "So shall your descendants be" that he
looked up into the stars, saw their vastness, their
multitude, and relaxed—resting in faith upon the
power of God.

If we focus our view on Abram's faith, we are going
to miss the point of this whole matter. Sometimes we
make far too much of these men and their faith.
"What mighty men of faith," we say; "how

tremendous to believe God against all the evidence of
the circumstances around. If we only had faith like
that we could do the things they did!" Then we compare our feeble faith with theirs and try to work up a
feeling of faith within us until we are turned into
spiritual hypochondriacs, always going about taking
our spiritual temperature and feeling our spiritual
pulse. It is indeed true that when God saw Abram's
faith, it was reckoned to him for righteousness; but it
is also true that when Abram saw God, he reckoned
him able to perform what he had promised, and so
was able to rest his faith on God's adequacy.

What was it that made his faith so strong? The answer is that he did not look at the difficulty so much
as he looked at the One who had promised. His eye
was not resting on the problems, but upon the Prom-
iser. When he saw the greatness of God, the might
and majesty displayed before him on that oriental
summer's night, he said to himself, "It makes no difference how I feel, nor what may be the difficulties
involved. The Creator of that multitude of stars is
quite capable of giving me an equal number of descendants."

> *Faith, mighty faith, the promise sees*
> *And looks to God alone,*
> *Laughs at impossibilities,*
> *And cries, "It shall be done!"*

So we read the great sentence, "He believed God
and it was reckoned to him for righteousness." This
does not mean this was the first moment that Abram
was reckoned righteous before God— that is, this is
not the moment of his spiritual regeneration. The
book of Hebrews makes clear that when he left Ur of
the Chaldees, in response to God's command, his
obedient faith was also reckoned to him for right-

eousness. This incident under the stars is simply one instance out of many which illustrates the way in which God reckons righteousness to the man who believes. Abram did not attain righteous standing by his own works, but when he rested in helpless dependence upon the might of God to do what he had promised. Then he won immediate favor in God's sight and the righteousness of Christ was imputed to him. Abram believed God about the promise of a coming son, and was reckoned righteous by faith.

Today we are exhorted to believe God about the Son who has already come; and when we cease our own works and rest in helpless dependence upon that living Son, we too are counted righteous by faith. That act of faith which first introduces us to the power of God, exercised on our behalf, must become an attitude of faith governing each moment of our life. Do not think you have come to the end of the road when you believe in Jesus Christ. You are then standing at the beginning, and every experience of the power of God in your life must be freshly appropriated by faith in the promise of God.

What wonderful lessons come to us from this book and these lives of men of old! How wonderful that in this twentieth century we may discover this same truth and be children of Abraham today. O, that we would learn the folly of self-dependence and the glory of God-dependence! In every moment of fear, we must cast ourselves upon Almighty God, reckoning upon his promise to be our shield and our exceeding great reward.

7
THE FURNACE
AND THE LAMP
(Genesis 15:7-21)

Students learning how to write in the country schoolhouses of old commonly used a copybook. Under a sample line of handwriting, every student laboriously tried to reproduce the original. It is not hard to tell who learned to write by this method, for they all have the same general style. The relationship between the Old and New Testaments is something like this. The Old Testament's record of how God dealt with Israel forms a sort of copybook which the New Testament uses as a pattern.

In our study of Abraham, we see the initial scriptural account of God's dealings with Israel. We recognize these stories are patterns of faith for the

believer today. What literally and physically occurred to Abraham occurs spiritually in the Christian's life. That is what makes these stories so eter-
nally fascinating and beneficial. This is why early
Christians, with nothing more than the Old Testament in their hands, could test and prove the doctrine of the apostles and other leaders. True teachings
from God only repeat on a higher level the pattern set
down in the Old Testament.

Genesis 15 condenses for us the whole doctrinal
movement of Romans 4-8. Since this is one of the
most important sections in the entire New Testament, this is also a highly important period in
Abraham's life. It begins with that great principle
which governed Abram's life—daily trusting that
God was able to do through him what he had promised. By this Abram was counted righteous when he
had no righteousness of his own. Paul clearly presents
this in Romans 4-5.

The following chapters, 6-8, explain how to be delivered from the reigning power of sin. If our Christian experience ends in Romans 4-5, we are of all men
most miserable, for we have not really entered into
the fullness that Christ purchased for us. We need to
learn by experience the process of sanctification,
taught in Romans 6-8 and beautifully pictured for us
in verses 7- 21 of this fifteenth chapter of Genesis. It
begins with nothing else but *heart hunger.*

> *And he said to him, "I am the LORD who brought*
> *you from Ur of the Chaldeans, to give you this*
> *land to possess." But he said, "O LORD God, how*
> *am I to know that I shall possess it?" (Genesis*
> *15:7-8).*

God reminded Abram that he was the one who had
called him to leave Ur and go into the land of Canaan.

Abram's response was, "LORD, how shall I know that
this land will be mine? I have been here now for ten
years. I have walked up and down the length and
breadth of it, as you told me to do. I have enjoyed
portions of it, but I don't get any of it. LORD, how
can I own the land that you said you would give to
me?" This shows the great desire in Abram's heart to
possess what God has offered him. It is his by promise, but he longs to make it his by ownership.

The land is both literal and spiritual. Abram is to
possess the literal land through his descendents, his
natural seed. But through his spiritual descendants
he is to fully possess the land symbolically. This is
the fullness of life in the Spirit; all that God intends
us to have in Jesus Christ, all the victory, the power,
the abundance, and the fruitfulness that comes by the
Holy Spirit. It is already ours by promise because we
belong to Jesus Christ. But the question is, have we
possessed it? Do we own it? Have we experienced it?
If not, our question must be that of Abram: how can
we make it fully ours?

Do you hunger for this land? Do you long to have
what God offers you? Abram says, "LORD God, how
can I know that I shall possess it?" He wants to learn
how God's promise to him will be fulfilled. His question comes not from unbelief or doubt, but from
wanting to know more. It is like Mary's question
when the angel Gabriel told her she was to have a
child: "How can I have a child when I am a virgin?"
This is not unbelief, but wonder concerning the process. So is Abram's question, and God answers him
by saying, in effect, "Come along, Abram, and I will
show the whole procedure to you. I will reveal the
means by which you, through your descendants, will
possess the land."

He begins by showing Abram that the first step must consider death!

> He said to him, "Bring me a heifer three years old, a she-goat three years old, a ram three years old, a turtledove, and a young pigeon." And he brought him all these, cut them in two, and laid each half over against the other; but he did not cut the birds in two. And when birds of prey came down upon the carcasses, Abram drove them away (Genesis 15:9-11).

Each of these creatures pictures Christ, our sacrifice. Our deliverance from the reigning power of sin must be based upon that sacrifice of Jesus Christ upon the cross. This is what we learn in Romans 6. We are told that Christ died for our sins in Romans 1-3. We learn that he died for sin in Romans 6. The perfect character of Christ—especially as it was poured out in death for us so that we might have real life—is illustrated for us by these animals and birds Abram brought. There on the cross something took place that can break the control and dominion of sin over us and allow the Holy Spirit to produce the character of Christ in us.

The heifer or ox symbolizes patience and strength. Who does not need these qualities! The she-goat is a symbol of nourishment and refreshment. The ram pictures power, might in warfare. The birds speak of gentleness and grace, the Spirit of God at work. It is significant that all the animals were to be three years old. This reminds us of the public ministry of our Lord, which lasted for three years. All these qualities of his character were publicly proclaimed during that time. Here, then, is a symbolic portrait of Jesus Christ in the beauty and full vigor of his manhood.

All that he was was clearly told out and made evident by his life.

All that Christ is was made available to us in his death. He laid down his life that we might have it! He poured out his soul unto death that all his fullness might indwell my life and yours, that we might have all that he is. The slaying of these animals and birds and Abram's long contemplation of them pictures all this for us.

Whether we view the land as literal or symbolic, we begin to possess it by thoroughly understanding what Christ has done to make possession possible. On the cross, our Lord won the right to own all the kingdoms of the earth. Some day the old hymn will be fulfilled, "Jesus shall reign where 'ere the sun does his successive journeys run." Israel, occupying the land of Palestine, will then be the chief of nations. It shall fully possess the land in accordance with the promise to Abram. This is equally true on the spiritual level. On the cross, the Lord won the right to fully possess the kingdom of the heart. It is no longer a matter of my struggling to do the best I can (which is never good enough). A life is available to me that can make me all I need and ought to be.

All day long Abram sat and watched the sacrificed animals, waiting . . . waiting . . . all through the long hot hours, considering what all this meant. When satanic doubts, as vultures, descended to rob him of blessing, he drove them away. That is what we must do when doubts beset us concerning the work of Christ. All day long Abram watched and waited, and out of his long contemplation there came the next step:

> *As the sun was going down, a deep sleep fell on Abram; and lo, a dread and great darkness fell*

*upon him. Then the LORD said to Abram, "Know
of a surety that your descendants will be sojourners
in a land that is not theirs, and will be slaves
there, and they will be oppressed for four hundred
years; but I will bring judgment on the nation
which they serve, and afterward they shall come
out with great possessions. As for yourself, you
shall be buried in a good old age. And they shall
come back here in the fourth generation; for the iniquity of the Amorites is not yet complete" (Genesis
15:12-16).*

As the sun touches the western horizon Abram
sinks into sleep, and there comes upon him a great
sense of horror and darkness. In the midst of it he is
given a revelation of the oppression and enslavement
of his descendants. This, as we know, was fulfilled to
the very letter. His descendants *did* go down into
Egypt (a land that was not theirs), and there they
were oppressed, afflicted, and enslaved for the length
of time recorded here. Then, at last, God sent Moses
to lead them out; Pharaoh and Egypt were judged;
and Israel was brought back into the land of Canaan—all exactly as God had told Abram. With this
revelation there is a personal word of encouragement
to Abram: he would not enter into this directly himself, but only his descendants would suffer these
things.

Note here the revelation of God's great patience.
He tells Abram that Israel must remain in Egypt for
four hundred years because the iniquity of the Amo-
rite tribes living in Canaan was "not yet full." That
is, these vicious tribes were to be allowed to run the
full course of their iniquity. All the depravity of their
hearts was to be allowed to express itself to the full,
so there could be no question of the righteousness of

God in judgment. When Israel at last came into the land again, they were commanded to exterminate all of these people—male and female, adult and child alike. Skeptics have used this to caricature God as exceedingly cruel. But the whole picture is of a God who waits patiently until these tribes degenerate into a moral cancer threatening to infect the nations around, requiring their removal. Archaeologists have given us glimpses into the moral life of these people, and it is incredibly foul. They indulged in fiendish rites in their worship, and their moral lives were polluted beyond description.

Spiritually, this is a picture of the implacable tyranny of self in the human heart. When we seriously contemplate the cross of Christ, we see our own enslavement to sin and self within. So many Christians fancy themselves free simply because they have received Christ. They may acknowledge a few minor weaknesses—a fit of temper now and then, an occasional display of jealousy, a little lust, a tendency toward stubbornness or willfulness—but these are minor peccadilloes we must all learn to live with. They look down their noses at the unregenerate and unwashed who have not yet come to Christ. Nevertheless, they are bothered with a sense of guilt and weakness which they do not understand. Then, gradually, they begin to see that they are mastered by self, that their choices are all made with self in view. Ego, as an ugly monster, sits on the throne of their lives; and though they pay lip service to the cause of Christ, self rules, cracking a remorseless whip and driving them to ever more selfishness.

This is the self-revelation which Paul describes in Romans 7:24: "Wretched man that I am! Who will deliver me from this body of death?" When this is our cry, we have begun to realize that we are, indeed, under the dominion of sin. We become aware of barrenness, fruitless activity, purpose without power, effort without effect. Our service becomes a job without joy. Worship is routine and mechanical. Life is a horror and great darkness. We wonder what is wrong, and cry out, "Who shall deliver me from this reigning power of self in my life?" It is right at this point that a new thing occurs—a vision and victory:

> When the sun had gone down and it was dark, behold, a smoking fire pot and a flaming torch passed between these pieces. On that day the LORD made a covenant with Abram, saying, "To your descendants I give this land, from the river Euphrates, the land of the Kenites, the Kenizzites, the Kadmonites, the Hittites, the Perizzites, the Rephaim, the Amorites, the Canaanites, the Girgashites and the Jebusites" (Genesis 15:17-21).

At the place of self-despair there comes deliverance! When we realize how much we are enslaved by selfishness, how little we really experience what God is offering, how much we are victims of our own self-indulgence, self-pity, and self-righteousness— then we are ready for victory. At the moment when the heart is cold and empty and the light of faith has gone out, something will precipitate a crisis, and suddenly you find yourself, without warning, in the midst of a smoking furnace.

When Jacob met his brother Esau he turned aside by the brook Peniel, and there the angel of God met and wrestled with him until he was broken. When David sat on his throne, Nathan the prophet came to tell him the story of an injustice in his kingdom. Suddenly, out of that story, there comes an arrow to the heart of David: "Thou art the man!" Instantly he recognized his plight in the smoking furnace.

Paul, newly converted, is filled with desire to be the apostle to Israel. He looks upon himself as the chosen vessel by which God intends to reach that people and bring them to Christ. With confidence he preaches in the city of Damascus. But suddenly events take a turn for the worse. No one will listen to him. At last he must be let down over the wall in a basket at night like a common criminal. That began the smoking furnace in his life.

Perhaps with you it may be a family crisis, a Bible conference, a trip away from home. Something precipitates a crisis, and you become aware that God is speaking to you and there is no way to escape his voice. He is putting his finger on the wrong thing in your life. He is going through your life like a furnace—searing, scorching, cleansing—and you cannot escape. You must face yourself. You have to acknowledge, judge, and reject yourself.

The instant you do, God is no longer a furnace but a lamp! You see everything clearly in a wonderful, illuminating light. What was confusing before is as clear as daylight now. You know what you have to do and you know how to go about doing it. Your true enemy is clearly defined. There before your eyes you see the Hittites, the Amorites, the Perizzites, and the Canaanites— all those filthy tribes that inhabit the human heart. You see that you have been defending and protecting them, though they have been defiling and polluting you. Bitterness, insensitivity, impatience, envy, self-righteousness, laziness, lust— these are the enemies you see.

But you also begin to see that Jesus Christ is more than all of them, that he is adequate for them, and that you can stand up in the strength of the Lord and smite these enemies and they will flee. You see plainly in his death that you died with him to these

sins and can now refuse them place in your thoughts.
You will find Christ has taken their place, and that in
the fullness of grace and truth he becomes to you
everything that you need— your wisdom, your
righteousness, your strength, and redemption. Suddenly you discover you are possessing the land! There
is joy and peace in your heart. Something new has
come in. You own what God has offered you. You
have found the way of deliverance. Joy, peace, grace,
glory—all now flood your heart.

This is the whole story of the Christian life after
conversion—a furnace and a lamp. That is the story
of the nation Israel throughout its history. It is a story
of affliction followed by blessing. First Israel is in the
furnace, and then the lamp is shining on them again.
At present they are in the furnace and have been for
nineteen hundred years, for they will not judge
themselves. But the Scriptures say they will soon
come to the place where, in the heat of the furnace,
they will cry out for deliverance and God will become
a lamp to them once again.

Christians will find this true for them personally.
Once you begin to set foot on the land of Spirit-given
power, you discover Jesus Christ is always a furnace
or a lamp. When self begins to threaten, he is a furnace—burning, scorching, searing. When self is
judged he immediately becomes a lamp, flooding the
whole life with radiance and glory. Have you made
this discovery? Have you found your way to this land
of promise? The one thing Abram had to do was
hunger for it. "Blessed are those who hunger and
thirst for righteousness, for they shall be satisfied"
(Matthew 5:6). When we long for this blessing and
freedom, then it is translated from mere theology
into experience.

As you may have discovered, it is quite possible to be an expert in teaching about spiritual adjustment but know nothing of its reality. It is not enough to *believe* in the doctrine of human depravity. There must come a time when you acknowledge the slavery of sin in *your* life, a time when *you* have groaned and turned in disgust from the revelation God has given you of your own heart. Only then can there come the wonderful release, the glorious deliverance, the satisfying sight of watching Canaanites flee before you. Habits you could not conquer before are now mastered in the strength of the Lord, and a whole new land of victory lies open before you.

Begin where Abram began. Say, "LORD God, how shall I know that I shall possess it? Reveal to me my own heart, and thy deliverance."

The transformed life of a Christian living in the strength of God is the most amazing, most revolutionary thing this world has ever seen. How much we need this today! May the Lord make us into people like this, that we may sing anew the songs of the early church, that we may know once again the transforming grace of the power of the Spirit in our lives, the impact that life can make upon life as we rub shoulders with those who do not yet know Christ. Let us not be content to live on the edge of the land, or merely to sojourn in it; but may we be restless until we own it, until we possess it in Jesus' name.

8
IT ALL
DEPENDS ON ME

(Genesis 16)

This record of the life of Abram was not written merely to recite historical facts from the distant past. Much of Christian Education is superficial in that it is concerned more with the mileage from Jericho to Jerusalem than with the distance between the lostness of man and the heart of God. Though we find the physical details of Abram's life interesting, we are much more concerned with their spiritual significance. To read the Old Testament in this way makes every page glow with color and light from God.

In chapter 16 of Genesis, God begins to translate what he has shown Abram in visions into the practical experience of his life. He does this also with us.

We catch sight of great things out of the Word and
grasp them intellectually, but then they must become a part of us through experience and get down
into our hearts where they affect and change us. It is
one thing to pass an examination on the process and
methods of the spiritual life; it is quite another to
pass God's examination of the degree to which we
have translated this knowledge into daily living. We
shall see here that although Abram had been
thoroughly instructed through the visions he received, yet he needed sad experience to teach him the
power of the self-life within and his need for the daily
power of the cross of Christ.

In chapter 16, verse 1, we read:

Now Sarai, Abram's wife, bore him no children.

After all the lofty experiences of his visions, this
was the heart-breaking fact to which Abram returned. For ten years he had been awaiting the fulfillment of God's promise. Sarai was by this time almost
seventy-five years old. Still there was no son. Despite
renewed promises, Abram was puzzled and discouraged by Sarai's barrenness.

This is also our problem in the life of faith. Like
Abram, we too are justified by faith. We accepted
this gift of God's righteousness by a simple act of our
will. We know we possess it, not by our efforts, but
by our faith in Jesus Christ. Then we set about trying
to please God because we are his. We do it by the only
means we know—trying to do the best we can. But
we discover quickly that somehow our Christianity
loses its glow and fire, and instead of the fruit of love,
joy, and peace which we were led to expect, we find
instead nothing but barrenness.

We have the same problem Abram had. This life
which is expected to produce immediate fruit results

only in barrenness. It is hard to understand. We find
no effectiveness in our lives. We are not enjoying
Christ as we once did. This is reflected in some of our
hymns. We sing:

> *Where is the blessedness we had,*
> *When first we knew the Lord?*

We look back to that first experience because our
present one has grown cold and does not produce the
joy, the glory, the glow and vigor that we expected.
We are trying our best, but something is wrong.
Sarai is barren, and there is no fruit as God had promised.

When the problem of barrenness begins to haunt
us, the next thing is inevitable: the proposal of the
flesh to do something about it!

> *She had an Egyptian maid whose name was*
> *Hagar; and Sarai said to Abram, "Behold now,*
> *the LORD has prevented me from bearing children;*
> *go in to my maid; it may be that I shall obtain*
> *children by her." And Abram hearkened to the*
> *voice of Sarai. So, after Abram had dwelt ten*
> *years in the land of Canaan, Sarai, Abram's*
> *wife, took Hagar the Egyptian, her maid, and*
> *gave her to Abram her husband as a wife (Genesis*
> *16:1-3).*

There is much in this action of Sarai which seems
praiseworthy. It was, first of all, an act of genuine and
costly sacrifice. She evidently said something like
this to herself: "God has promised my husband a son,
through whom he means to fulfill all his promises.
Yet he has never said that the son must come through
me, and perhaps he means to fulfill this promise
another way." So she resolves (through what
struggles we can only imagine) to give up her own

rights in an act of courageous renunciation. She gives
up a wife's most precious possession—the right to
have her husband's sole affection—and she offers her
maid to her husband that he might have a child by
her and thus fulfill the will of God.

Abram was, as we know, a monogamist. That is
not the same as monotonous! He had only one wife,
and he was quite content with that arrangement. But
to give him the son of his heart's desire, Sarai was
willing to sacrifice that relationship. It was not only
an act of real sacrifice, but also one of deep sincerity.
She did not hope that he would talk her out of it. She
was quite prepared to go through with it, cost what
it may. She took the initiative in proposing it.

Furthermore, it was a socially acceptable act,
strange as that may seem to us. There was nothing
immoral about it in the eyes of the community. This
was common in the life of these nomadic people.
Many of the Canaanite leaders would have had more
than one wife, and neither Abram nor Sarai would be
less highly regarded because of it. No one would
laugh at her, nor point the finger of scorn. It was a
perfectly proper act in the eyes of the community.

Yet, as we see the end of this action, it was an act
of appalling folly and stupidity which resulted in
endless sorrow and heartache. The results are evident
yet, four thousand years later! The Arab nations
originated in this act, and the enmity which sprang
up between Israel and the Arabs (descendants of
Ishmael) troubles the world to this day. If ever we
have a picture of the longevity of sin, it is here. Despite the seeming rightness of this to Sarai, it was the
worst thing she could have done.

But what was wrong with it? How could Sarai have
known what the results would be? How can we blame
her for her decision? Here we need to go very slowly

and listen very carefully. We are so like Sarai ourselves that we resent the idea that she should be blamed for this. Yet if we do not learn the lesson here, we shall find our own Christian lives continually plagued with this problem of barrenness, and we shall miss the secret of victory and fruitfulness. Here in a picture is the great secret Paul labors to develop in Galatians: how to walk in the Spirit and not fulfill the lusts of the flesh. He uses this very incident to illustrate it. *deny self—when the choice arises...*

Sarai's trouble was simply that all her actions grew out of a philosophy which, very simply, says: "God has told me what he wants, now the rest of it is up to me. God has shown me what the goal is, but it is up to me to figure out how to reach it. I know what he wants, and I can count on him for help; but the rest is up to me." This is the philosophy which led to all the folly and heartache and sorrow that plagued Abram and Sarai. Many others have followed them in the centuries since then.

You will recognize at once that this is a common and widespread idea. We continually think and act this way in the church. We say the reason God's work is not going forward as it should is that we are not trying hard enough. We are barren because we have not really put ourselves into this. Let us hold some more committee meetings. Let's get going. It all depends on us!

We find in our Bibles what we call "the Great Commission:" "Go into all the world and preach the gospel to the whole creation" (Mark 16:15). This is the goal he wants us to fulfill, we say; now the rest is up to us. We must plan all the strategy, we must raise the money and determine where it will be spent, we must convince candidates that they should go. It is all up to us.

And many times we *do* get some fruit from this. We get results. We hold our meetings, plan our programs, put on our pressures . . . and we get results. But, oh, are they unsatisfactory! Do you know why? We've gotten Ishmael instead of Isaac!

We hear our Lord say in the first chapter of Acts, "You shall be witnesses," and every truly Christian heart says, "All right, Lord, this is what you want me to do—I will do it." We never bother to find out how he wants it done, or whether he has a program to carry it out. We start out in fleshly zeal and pass out tracts to everyone we meet. We buttonhole people at meetings. When it all fails, we recognize that something is wrong, and we wring our hands and quit. We say, "I've tried to obey the Lord, but it doesn't work, so I quit!"

We read in Scripture that we should have elders in every church, and that God's plan is to direct his church through these men. So we hold an election and put up the wealthiest members or the most popular ones. These men then run the church as they would a business, stumbling on in total disregard of the living Head who is completely capable of running his own church. We never bother to find out how he makes known to us the men of his choice, and how he proposes to declare his will through them. So we have a church filled with divisions and strife, and realize we have Ishmael on our hands instead of Isaac.

Perhaps the worst thing of all—and certainly the matter before us in the story of Abram and Sarai—is that in reading Scripture we learn we are supposed to be conformed to the image of Christ. So we set out to be like Jesus. We make up a list of rigid rules for acceptable behavior. We become frightfully busy doing things for God. We work our fingers to the bone, and spend hour after hour in the church, neglecting our family, our own life, and everything else in order to do things for the Lord. We sincerely try to meet his demands. We do our best. We note how the community around approves our strenuous efforts and pats us on the back for our faithful spirit. But despite all the effort and sincerity, deep in our hearts we know there is nothing but barrenness. Or if there is fruit, it is not the kind we wanted. It is forced, unnatural, sustained only by continual effort. We fall far short of the image of Christ.

This was what happened to Sarai. Note the sacrifice, the seemliness, the appearance of selflessness. The result is fruit, all right. But it is Ishmael, not Isaac; the fruit of the flesh rather than of the Spirit. In some moment of illumination we ask, "Why are we so barren? Why so unfruitful? Where is the impact, the power? What has become of the glow, that living vitality we see in the early Christians? What is wrong?" It is all a result of failing to learn God's *way* as well as his *will*.

In verse two we read, "Abram hearkened to the voice of Sarai and went in to Hagar the Egyptian." Abram was more culpable than Sarai. She acted in relative ignorance, but he knew better. We are specifically told that he had dwelt ten years in the land of Canaan, learning every day that God is sufficient for every need. He should have learned that God knows what he is doing and is quite capable of administering and carrying out his plans. He had observed God's methods for ten years; he should have been a steadying influence upon Sarai here. But instead he hearkened to her and went in to Hagar. It is the story of Adam and Eve all over again.

There are three obvious mistakes that lay behind Abram's act. First, he listened to the voice of one who was not as far along in the spiritual life as he was. This is a frequent source of failure today. What may seem right to young Christians may be terribly wrong for you, simply because you are at a different level or stage of spiritual growth. We must ever be careful of taking advice from someone who is younger in spiritual things than ourselves. This is why the Spirit of God warns against placing men in church leadership who are novices. It is not enough to have the gifts of the Spirit which equip one for leadership; there must also be a cumulative experience of time and spiritual growth, making possible wise direction.

Abram's second mistake was that he consented to something that especially harmonized with the desires of his self-life. Take care here! He longed for a son, and the longing, though proper, made him too ready to find a way to satisfy it. When some advice is particularly amenable to something you want very much, be careful. It may be nothing more than pleasing the self-life, as it was here.

The third mistake, the one he shared with Sarai, was his readiness to do the will of God without seeking to discover the way of God. Here is the heart of the problem. This is the most serious error of Christians today. Hudson Taylor said, "God's work, done in God's way, will never lack God's supply." And the entire record of the China Inland Mission proves it.

All through Scripture there is incident after incident to illustrate the folly of being committed to the will of God without being committed to his way. Young Moses graduated from the University of Egypt with his diploma in hand, a doctor of philosophy in the humanities. Burning in his heart was a great crusade. He knew he was the chosen instrument by which God planned to deliver the people of Israel from the bondage and slavery in which they lived. The first thing he saw was an Egyptian beating an Israelite. He said to himself, "Ah, this is my opportu-

Title: "look b4 u leap."
Kids

nity. Here is a slave being mistreated. I have a commission and mandate from God to deliver these slaves, and this is my chance to start." So he looked about to see if any man was watching (though it never occurred to him that God was looking), slew the Egyptian and hid his body in the sand.

The next day he arose early and said to himself, "Yesterday I got a good start on the job God gave me, so today I'll go out and see who else I can deliver." He found two Israelites arguing, and he stepped up and said, "God has appointed me your judge, so let me hear this case." They said to him, "Wait a minute. Who appointed you to judge us? Are you going to kill us like you did that Egyptian yesterday?" Those words sent a great fear sweeping over Moses and he turned and ran into the wilderness. He had to flee Egypt. Why? Because he was trying in the strength of the flesh to do the will of God. For forty years his life was a burned-out desert of barrenness, until he learned at last the secret of yielding himself to the control of God's Spirit. He had to learn to do God's work in God's way.

Now back to the record of Abram's folly. We have seen what the proposal of the flesh looked like; now we must see the petulance that follows:

> *And he went in to Hagar, and she conceived; and when she saw that she had conceived, she looked with contempt on her mistress. And Sarai said to Abram, "May the wrong done to me be on you! I gave my maid to your embrace, and when she saw that she had conceived, she looked on me with contempt. May the LORD judge between you and me!" But Abram said to Sarai, "Behold, your maid is in your power; do to her as you please." Then Sarai dealt harshly with her, and she fled from her (Genesis 16:4-6).*

The immediate results of acting in the flesh are always the same. We become petty and petulant, displaying enmity, strife, jealousy, anger, selfishness, and other ugly emotions which lie ever near the surface of the fallen human heart. Wherever these appear, they are the thermometer which tells us we are being ruled by the self and not by the Spirit. Here they are in this account, as contemporary as today's newspaper.

The first one mentioned is *contempt*. When Abram placed Hagar into rivalry with his wife, Sarai, Hagar become insolent and impertinent and held her mistress in utter contempt, taunting her about her barrenness. She forced Sarai to drink the gall of bitterness.

The next step is *unreasonableness*. Sarai said to Abram, "May the wrong done to me be on you." If you have had any doubts that Sarai was a real woman, this will convince you! She initiated the proposal to Abram; she urged it upon him. But when he gave in, she turned and threw it back in his face, crying, "It's all your fault! Why did you do this to me? May the LORD judge between you and me." This woman is mad clear through! That is what Laban said to Jacob when they parted from each other in anger (Genesis 31:53). What it means is, "The LORD keep you from sticking a dagger in my back, and keep me from sticking one in yours, while we are unable to keep our eyes on each other." That is what it means here. "May the LORD keep his eye on you, you scoundrel! Look what you've done." How completely unreasonable— but how completely characteristic of the flesh.

Then the next symptom is *irresponsibility*. Abram said to Sarai, "Behold, the maid is in your power; do to her as you please." If you had any doubts that Abram was a real man, this should convince you! He is dodging his responsibility, passing the buck. "Don't bother me with this," he says, "it is your problem—you settle it."

The result is harshness and rebellion. "Sarai dealt harshly with her, and she fled from her." Do you know this pattern? The whole household is in an uproar by now. Yet every one of them could have said piously, "We were only trying to do the will of the LORD." Each one is sure the others are wholly to blame; no one is willing to face the evil of his own heart. There is a strong implication at the beginning of the next chapter that this unhappy state of affairs went on for thirteen long years. All this is a result of trying to help God when it seemed that perhaps he had tackled a job too hard for him, or that time would run out before it could be accomplished. We know the will of God; let us also decide his way.

In the last section of the chapter, we see the provision of God's grace:

> *The angel of the LORD found {Hagar} by a spring of water in the wilderness, the spring on the way to Shur. And he said, "Hagar, maid of Sarai, where have you come from and where are you going?" She said, "I am fleeing from my mistress Sarai." The angel of the LORD said to her, "Return to your mistress, and submit to her." The angel of the LORD also said to her, "I will so greatly multiply your descendants that they cannot be numbered for multitude." And the angel of the LORD said to her, "Behold, you are with child, and shall bear a son; you shall call his name Ishmael; because the LORD has given heed to your affliction. He shall be a wild ass of a man, his hand against every man and every man's hand against him; and he shall dwell over against all*

his kinsmen." So she called the name of the LORD
who spoke to her, "Thou art a God of seeing"; for
she said, "Have I really seen God and remained
alive after seeing him?" Therefore the well was
called Beer-la-hai-roi; it lies between Kadesh and
Bered. And Hagar bore Abram a son; and Abram
called the name of his son, whom Hagar bore,
Ishmael. Abram was eighty-six years old when
Hagar bore Ishmael to Abram (Genesis 16:7-
16).

It is "the angel of the LORD" who finds Hagar.
This is the first appearance of this phrase in Scripture,
and as we compare it with other uses, we find that
this refers to none other than the preincarnate Christ.
This is the Son of God himself, appearing to Hagar.
He says four things to her.

First, "Where do you come from and where are you
going?" These are always arresting questions. Hagar
answers the first, but she has nothing to say to the
last. She does not know where she is going. Where
can she go? The question draws her helplessness
sharply to her attention.

Then the angel says, "Return and submit." This is
the only way to experience the grace and blessing of
God. Had she gone on wandering into the wilderness, disaster awaited. Both she and the child in her
womb would have died. When God finds us wandering, this is always what he says: "Return and submit." "Submit to the circumstances you dislike, and
I will work it out. To do anything else is folly." So
Hagar returns.

With the command to return comes the promise
of blessing. Blessing always follows obedience. "I
will multiply your descendants so that they cannot
be numbered for multitude." And then follows the

prophecy of Ishmael's nature. "He shall be a wild ass of a man, his hand against every man and every man's hand against him." He will be a non-conformist, a Missouri mule—a man whom no one can get along with.

The spiritual significance of this is explained in Galatians 4. There Paul says that Hagar is a picture of the law, and Ishmael, her son, pictures those who try to establish favor in God's sight through religious activity. These are the Ishmaelites, and God says there shall be a great multitude, more than any man can number. Spiritually it is written of them, "Those who are in the flesh cannot please God."

Hagar, glimpsing here something of God's omniscience and power, names him, "The God Who Sees," for she says, "Have I even here seen him who sees me?" This event gripped her. "Here is a God who sees me and knows me just as I am, and all that concerns me." So she named the well, "The well of One who lives and sees." (It is named after God, not after her, as the RSV suggests.) Have you found God to be the One who lives and sees, the One who knows all about your life and your circumstances? The One who knows the past and the future, and says to you as he said to Hagar, "Return and submit"? That is the place of promised blessing.

We are also told that this well is located between Kadesh and Bered. Kadesh means "holiness" and Bered means "hail" or "judgment." Here is a well of grace, lying between holiness and judgment. When we begin to stray from the place of God's blessing toward the certainty of judgment, God meets us on the way, at the well of grace, saying, "Now wait a minute. I don't want to have to make this known to others. I don't want to judge you openly. I don't want to bring trial or affliction or heartache into your life to make you listen. Listen now. Return and submit so I won't have to do this." That is the well of grace.

So Hagar returns and Ishmael is born. We read nothing about Abram for thirteen years. The next chapter opens when he is ninety-nine years old. This means that for thirteen years, strife, disagreement, bitterness, jealousy, and heartache characterized that tent in the land of Canaan. It is God's way of teaching Abram: ". . . for apart from me you can do nothing" (John 15:5). It does not depend on us, it all depends on him. We need constantly to reassert our utter dependence upon the God who knows us, knows our circumstances, knows our problems, and who is completely able to work through us to accomplish all that he desires.

How many mistakes we have made by doing this very thing that we have seen Abram do! Let us ask the Lord to forgive us our consummate folly and to teach us—as he taught Abram—to walk in the Spirit in dependence upon him alone. We must come to the place where we recognize the folly of our flesh and the impossibility of pleasing God in its strength. We must learn to do everything through constant and unrelenting reliance upon the Lord to work through us. In this way—and only in this way— shall we enjoy the same blessing and success that Abram eventually found.

9

THE
CIRCUMCISED
LIFE

(Genesis 17)

Up to this point we have been following Abram as
a believer in the true God, sojourning in the land of
promise. But the difference between a believer and a
circumcised believer is vital indeed, and it is to this
difference that the Spirit of God directs our attention
in Genesis 17.

Our last view of Abram found him attempting to
help God. He was trying to solve a problem he
thought far too hard for God. He and Sarai believed
they could solve the problem, and Abram took
Hagar, Sarai's handmaid, for a wife. Of that union
was born Ishmael, Israel's continual thorn in the flesh
until this day.

Thirteen years elapsed between the events of chapter 16 and those of chapter 17, and we can well suspect they were years of unhappiness and unrest in Abram's household. The presence of Ishmael in the home created endless contempt, bitterness, envy, jealousy, weariness of spirit, and rebellion. These thirteen years were designed by God to teach Abram the folly of acting on his own.

Perhaps you have had some similar experience, when God has allowed you to have your own way and the results were appalling. You were permitted to go your own headstrong way in order that you might learn the folly of acting apart from God. One of the most frightening things about life with God is this fact, that if you insist upon having your own way, he will often let you have it . . . until you are sorry you asked for it. "He gave them their request, but sent leanness into their souls" (Psalm 106:15 KJV).

After thirteen years of heartache, a new aspect of God's grace opens before Abram. Three new developments arise in chapter 17. The first is the new revelation he has of God:

> *When Abram was ninety-nine years old the LORD appeared to Abram, and said to him, "I am God Almighty; walk before me, and be blameless. And I will make my covenant between me and you, and will multiply you exceedingly" (Genesis 17:1,2).*

After thirteen years of silence, God appears to Abram in a new revelation and with a new name— God Almighty. In the Hebrew it is *El Shaddai*, which essentially means "the God who is sufficient," "the all-competent God," "the adequate God, who knows what he is doing and how to do it." This indicates that Abram has learned something from his recent bitter experience. God says in effect, "You have been learning for thirteen years the total inadequacy of your own efforts, through Ishmael. Now learn a new thing about me. I am El Shaddai. You have discovered by sad experience how futile your plans and efforts can be without me. Now learn how capable I am to do everything that I desire to do, whenever I desire to do it." Would that we all would discover this! We need desperately to recover the reality of El Shaddai, the God who is sufficient for whatever we are going through right now. This is what Abram learned.

In this new light from God came a new demand from God: "Walk before me and be blameless." In the King James Version this word "blameless" is translated "perfect." The root meaning of the word is "wholehearted." "Walk before me and be perfect, wholehearted," God says, "because I am El Shaddai." That is, I am all-sufficient to make you blameless. Walk before me, therefore, and be blameless.

I remember one time when I was a boy, I was looking through the iron bars of a large gate at a beautiful estate full of flower-bordered walks, and eyeing it with a great deal of envy. Suddenly, before I saw him, another boy about my own age rushed up from the other side and gave my arms a jerk. The bump I received taught me the foolishness of trying to be on two sides of a fence at once.

This is so often brought before us in the New Testament. We are so constantly trying to serve two masters, to please self and Christ. We are content to serve Christ, if at the same time we can also serve self. But God says to Abram, "This can no longer be permitted. You have come to the place where your dual allegiance can no longer be tolerated. Walk now before me, appropriating what I am, and be wholehearted, be wholly on my side, be mine!"

This is what a circumcised life means. It is Christ asserting his practical lordship in our lives. When you became a Christian, you did so by recognizing the right of Jesus Christ to be Lord in your life. You did not, of course, understand what that would involve. But you saw, in one way or another, that his willingness to save you involved his right to control you. For a time, though you knew you were essentially different, you lived much as you did before. You made decisions on the basis of how you felt and what you wanted to do. Then the Holy Spirit begins to put on the pressure. He says to you, "Stop this," or "Start doing that." All he is really doing is asserting the lordship of Christ in your life. He is beginning to cut the ties that bind you to the world and the self within you. This is essentially what he is saying to Abram here.

So important is this step, along with the new revelation of God, that new names are given to Abram and Sarai:

> Then Abram fell on his face; and God said to him, "Behold, my covenant is with you, and you shall be the father of a multitude of nations. No longer shall your name be Abram, but your name shall be Abraham; for I have made you the father of a multitude of nations" (Genesis 17:3-5).

And then in verse 15:

> And God said to Abraham, "As for Sarai your wife, you shall not call her name Sarai, but Sarah shall be her name. I will bless her, and moreover I will give you a son by her; I will bless her, and she shall be a mother of nations; kings of people shall come from her" (Genesis 17:15,16).

Whenever you see God in a new way, it always makes a corresponding change in you. Here God says to Abraham, "Look, Abram, your name now means 'exalted father.' Your trouble all along has been that you were looking for your own exaltation. This must now be changed. You must lose your desire to exalt yourself; you will stop trying to advance and please yourself. Your name will now be 'the father of a multitude,' for great fruitfulness shall be evident in your life. Because you have now learned that I am El Shaddai, your name can no longer be 'exalted' but it must now be 'fruitful,' for you will be the father of a multitude."

The same is true of Sarai. Sarai means "contentious." This speaks volumes about the home life of Abram and Sarai. In Proverbs 21:9, Solomon writes, "It is better to live in a corner of the housetop than in a house shared with a contentious woman." Having had a thousand wives, here is a man who knows of what he speaks! Sarai is, therefore, a problem wife. Yet in the New Testament, Peter says that this woman is a model for all women to follow—not by her name, Sarai, "contentiousness," but by her new name, Sarah, "Princess."

She is never referred to as Sarai in the New Testament. God does not set her up as a pattern for women until she becomes Sarah and loses her contentious spirit. As Sarah she learned to develop " . . . a gentle and quiet spirit, which in God's sight is very precious" (1 Peter 3:4). Sarai was not naturally thus. She was an argumentative woman, a nagging wife. But she, too, had been taught by grace, and through the years she lost the need to defend herself on every occasion. So she became Sarah, a princess, a queen, an honored woman, having a meek and quiet spirit, very precious in the sight of God.

Now we come to the great sign of circumcision:

And God said to Abraham, "As for you, you shall keep my covenant, you and your descendants after you throughout their generations. This is my covenant, which you shall keep, between me and you and your descendants after you: Every male among you shall be circumcised. You shall be circumcised in the flesh of your foreskins, and it shall be a sign of the covenant between me and you. He that is eight days old among you shall be circumcised; every male throughout your generations, whether born in your house, or bought with your money from any foreigner who is not of your offspring, both he that is born in your house and he that is bought with your money, shall be circumcised (Genesis 17:9-13).

And the actual event is recorded in verses 22-26:

When he had finished talking with him, God went up from Abraham. Then Abraham took Ishmael his son and all of the slaves born in his house or bought with his money, every male among the men of Abraham's house, and he circumcised the flesh of their foreskins that very day, as God had said to him. Abraham was ninety-nine years old when he was circumcised in the flesh of his foreskin. And Ishmael his son was thirteen years old when he was circumcised in the flesh of his foreskin. That very day Abraham and his son Ishmael were circumcised; and all the men of his house, those born in the house and those bought with money from a foreigner, were circumcised with him.

What a strange thing this is—the removal of the foreskin of the male procreative organ—literally carving in the flesh the sign of God's lordship! This is the great sign of Jewry, intended by God to be the mark of his possession, that they were God's instrument to use for blessing among the nations. It was placed upon this particular part of the body to indicate that they were to be physically separate from the other nations. The very organ by which that separation could be violated bore upon it the mark of God's ownership.

As we read the course of Jewish history, we see how this mark, intended to be the sign of humility and instrumentality, became perverted into a mark of superiority and favoritism. Those who bore it began to look on others as "Gentile dogs" and to be self-righteous and proud over their supposed favored position before God. Thus the spirit of anti-Semitism which so troubles the world today was born of the spirit of anti-Gentilism which preceded it. This does not justify either, of course.

Now let us remember that what was physical and literal to Abraham has spiritual significance to us. In the New Testament we no longer read of circumcision of the flesh, but of the heart. The heart is the symbol of the soul—the mind, emotions, and will, the whole personality. Every believer in Christ is to bear on his heart the sign of Christ's lordship. The total personality is to be at his disposal. That is the Christian's circumcised life.

Many scholars believe circumcision was the origin of the wedding ring. The act of circumcision was performed by a metal or stone knife which cut around the foreskin, leaving a circular scar. So a man and a woman, standing before someone who represents God, place a metal or stone ring upon each other's fingers, indicating that two hearts are giving themselves to each other.

This is the meaning of heart circumcision—the

believer's heart is totally Christ's, to use as he wills. All his emotions, mind, intellect, and will are dedicated and available, ready at the command of Jesus Christ to be used for his purposes. Paul says to the Philippians, "We are the circumcision, who worship God in the spirit and rejoice in Christ Jesus, and have no confidence in the flesh." We are not to rely upon ourselves, but depend totally upon him. Every thought, every imagination, is brought into captivity to Christ. That is the circumcised life.

"Walk therefore before me, and be wholehearted, blameless." That will be a life of fruitfulness and blessing, a life that is well-pleasing to God, for it all springs from realizing that the God who lives within is El Shaddai, the God who is sufficient.

10
WHEN
GOD COMES
TO DINNER

(Genesis 18:1-15)

In the last chapter we saw Abraham entering into the circumcised life. This pictures the heart that is wholly Christ's. Paul describes it this way in Philippians 3:3: "We are the true circumcision, who worship God in spirit, and glory in Christ Jesus, and put no confidence in the flesh." That is the circumcised life. Abraham, led by the Spirit of God through many difficulties and trials—and after years of wandering from victory to defeat and back again—has come into the fullness of the circumcised life.

In chapter 18 we shall see the practical results of this. Here is a homey scene, what we might call kitchen-sink religion. It is faith-in-overalls, a combination of grace and groceries. These few verses center around three persons. We first see God in disguise, then Abraham in haste, and finally, Sarah in doubt.

In the first five verses God appears in disguise:

> *And the LORD appeared to him by the oaks of Mamre, as he sat at the door of his tent in the heat of the day. He lifted up his eyes and looked, and behold, three men stood in front of him. When he saw them, he ran from the tent door to meet them, and bowed himself to the earth, and said, "My lord, if I have found favor in your sight, do not pass by your servant. Let a little water be brought, and wash your feet, and rest yourselves under the tree, while I fetch a morsel of bread, that you may refresh yourselves, and after that you may pass on—since you have come to your servant." So they said, "Do as you have said" (Genesis 18:1-5).*

We are told clearly in verse one who this is that appears to Abraham. "The LORD appeared to him by the oaks of Mamre." It is Yahweh himself coming to see Abraham, and with him come two angels who appear later on in connection with the destruction of Sodom. These are the same two who visit Lot to warn him of the impending judgment upon the cities of the plain. Because there are three men here, some have taken this to be a representation of the Trinity— Father, Son, and Holy Spirit. But a careful look at the context indicates that this is what we might regard as a preincarnate appearance of the second person of the Trinity, the Son of God, the Lord Jesus Christ. Here is one of those mysterious appearances of Christ before he came to take upon himself human flesh. He appears as a man, accompanied by two angels, in human disguise.

Abraham does not recognize him. All he sees is three travelers, weary and thirsty as they come in off the desert where the temperature often reaches 120-125 degrees in the shade—and there is no shade. Abraham is seated under the oaks of Mamre in the doorway of his tent in the heat of the day looking out on the blazing countryside. Suddenly he sees three men coming toward him. The salutation, "my Lord," with which Abraham addresses the central figure, is simply the common language of courtesy and does not mean he had any hint that this was indeed the LORD. You will notice in the Revised Standard Version that "lord" is not capitalized. This is correct. Further, Abraham's offer of food, rest, and water shows he had no idea whom he was entertaining.

This is obviously a test of Abraham's heart—whether he is really a circumcised believer—in which God appears in such a commonplace way that Abraham is not aware of his identity. I've long wished for some kind of a test which could be used in Bible schools and seminaries to determine how spiritually mature students have grown. Tests commonly used reveal only how much information has been mastered. There is little which reveals the real spiritual achievement of a life. It is quite possible, and in fact demonstrable, to graduate from seminary with a Doctor of Divinity degree or a doctorate in theology and not possess true spirituality or true maturity in Christ.

Nevertheless, although man has not been able to devise any such test, God is always testing us, and his testing does not come when we are warned and ready. Anyone can pass a test then. If I tell you that I am going to test you to see if you exhibit love under pressure, or whether you can keep your temper when

things are going wrong, you are likely to pass with
flying colors.

But God never tests that way. His tests catch us
unprepared, off-guard. It is when we are confronted
with some simple situation no one will know about
that the tests of life really come. When you are relaxing at home and the phone rings and suddenly you
are confronted with a call for help, or a demand for a
response—and you had planned to relax and enjoy
yourself all afternoon—what happens then? That's
the test.

When you are busy around the house with your
hands immersed in dishwater and something is burning on the stove and the refrigerator has just quit and
the sink is stopped up and you've got sixteen different
problems on your mind and your child comes up and
asks why it is that puppies bark but don't meow
while kitties meow but don't bark—what do you do
then? That's the test. When your neighbor or friend
gets sick and somebody has to take care of the children—what do you do? What is your reaction? These
are the tests of God. This is the way God tested
Abraham.

Is this not the meaning of Paul's words in Romans
12? "I appeal to you therefore, brethren . . . to present your bodies as a living sacrifice . . ." It is one
thing to be present in a great meeting where the
Spirit is moving in evident power and an appeal goes
out to rededicate the heart, and we hear the words,
"Present your bodies as living sacrifices unto the
Lord." Under the stress or pull of that meeting we
may well come up to the front and say, "Here am I
Lord, I give my life to you." But this is never the real
test. The test comes when some situation occurs in
daily life that forces you to face the question: Is my
body really available for him to do what he wants?

Am I ready to respond to the need of the human heart right there in front of me, right there at that moment? Am I ready to give of myself without stint and without limitation to meet a demand that comes suddenly in the course of my busy life? These are the true tests. This is what God is doing to Abraham when he appears without warning in the heat of the day.

Now let us see how Abraham fared:

> And Abraham hastened *into the tent to Sarah, and said, "Make ready quickly three measures of fine meal, knead it, and make cakes." And Abraham* ran *to the herd, and took a calf, tender and good, and gave it to the servant, who* hastened *to prepare it. Then he took curds, and milk, and the calf which he had prepared, and set it before them; and he stood by them under the tree while they ate (Genesis 18:6-8).*

How beautifully Abraham met his test! Look at the words of action here. He hastened into the tent and he said to her, "Make ready quickly three measures of fine meal." Then Abraham ran to the herd, picked out a calf, and gave it to the servant who hastened to prepare it. These words all indicate his prompt and ready response to the need before him.

He did it all personally, too. We know Abraham had more than 318 men in his household who were his servants, but here he himself becomes personally involved. He does not pass the buck; he hastens to do this himself. Sarah, too, is involved personally in making bread, although she also had servants. Hagar was there and others, but she herself makes this bread and kneads it and makes it into loaves.

When I read of Abraham's personal selection of the calf— tender and good—I remember something that occurred when I was with Dr. H.A. Ironside. Once

What wd u offer to G @ the dr?

at the close of a message, a dear old man came up to him and said, "Oh, Doctor, that was a wonderful message. It was just like Abraham's calf, tender and good." Dr. Ironside always thought that was one of the finest compliments he had ever received.

Abraham soon had a wonderful meal ready. He had cottage cheese salad (curds, it says) with figs cut up nicely in it; a tall glass of cool milk; hot veal cutlets, breaded and chicken- fried just the way they are the most tender; and fresh hot bread right out of the oven, running over with melted country butter; a nice dish of Sarah's preserves; and to top off the meal there was the gracious hospitality with which the guests were served. As they ate, Abraham visited with them.

All this beautifully pictures for us the fellowship of a circumcised heart with Christ in becoming his instrument to meet the cry of human need all around. The Lord said in Revelation 3:20, "Behold, I stand at the door and knock; if any one hears my voice and opens the door, I will come in to him and eat with him, and he with me." That is, we will fellowship together, we will have dinner together. This is not simply private enjoyment, not just a social hour for our own pleasure. When the Lord uses us as an instrument to meet the need of those around us, we enter into fellowship with the heart of Christ. When Christ comes in to us, he doesn't come in merely to give us a good time, to bless us, to make it an enjoyable experience. He comes in to fulfill his long-standing desire to be what he came into the world to be—a Savior to seek and to save that which was lost, to give and show compassion to others, to minister to human needs whatever they may be, through us.

Isn't this the test which he himself said he would apply to our lives? In Matthew 25 the Lord presents a scene of judgment (verses 31-43). He will divide the nations into two groups. They all claim to be his, but as he sees the human heart there are two divisions. He says to the one group (verse 41): "Depart from me, you cursed, into the eternal fire . . ." And they are amazed and say, "Why do you say that to us, Lord?" And he says, "for I was hungry and you gave me no food, I was thirsty and you gave me no drink, I was a stranger and you did not welcome me" (Matthew 25:42,43).

Then to the others, he will say (verse 34): " . . . Inherit the kingdom prepared for you from the foundation of the world." And they are surprised, too, and say, "Lord, what do you mean?" And he says, "for I was hungry and you gave me food, I was thirsty and you gave me drink, I was a stranger and you welcomed me, I was naked and you clothed me, I was sick and you visited me, I was in prison and you came to me" (Matthew 25:35,36).

And they reply in verse 39: "And when did we see you sick or in prison and visit you?" You remember his words: "Truly, I say to you, as you did it to one of the least of these my brethren, you did it to me" (Matthew 25:40).

This is the true test of our faith. James says:

> *Religion that is pure and undefiled before God and the Father is this: to visit orphans and widows in their affliction, and to keep oneself unstained from the world (James 1:27).*

As he so practically reminds us, faith that does not issue in this kind of a ministry is not real, saving faith; it does not work. The true test of our life is how much our hearts are yielded and wholly dedicated to Christ to respond in fellowship with him in the meeting of human need about us.

This test reveals that Abraham really has a circumcised heart. He is not doing this because he wants to gain something for himself. He is not trying to impress anybody. He is not seeking credit or recognition. He is not trying to display his piety. For all he knows these three men are nothing but poverty-stricken, penniless nomads of the desert. He will perhaps never see them again. But he treats them as royally as though they were kings. Even if he had known who they were, he could not have treated them better. This prompt and full response simply reflects a heart filled with grace and love, responding immediately to human need without thought of self or praise from others.

What made him do this? It was that he had a circumcised heart; he really was Christ's. The man who really is Jesus Christ's does not need to be talked into doing good deeds; rather he looks for opportunities. He is always ready to respond. Someone has well said, "Your reputation is what you do when everyone is looking, while your character is what you do when no one sees."

These tests come to us every day. When the need for help arises, what do you do about it? Do you run and hide or run to meet it as Abraham did here? I heard of a Christian who was speaking at a men's meeting some time ago about the growing spirit of callous indifference in the world today. He illustrated it by telling how he and a friend just a few days before had been walking through the busy streets of one of our cities when they saw a drunk lying in the street, half on the sidewalk. They noted how everybody was stepping over him and going on their way, paying no attention to the man. He said he was appalled at the indifference of people as they walked by.

"And you know," he said, "when we came back from lunch he was still there!"

How have you been doing this week with the sick, the hungry, the thirsty, the dying, the strangers, and those who need help physically or spiritually? What is your response? This is the question the Spirit thrusts upon us from this story.

The last picture applies to the feminine side of the household. Here we see Sarah in doubt:

> *They said to him, "Where is Sarah your wife?" And he said, "She is in the tent." The LORD said, "I will surely return to you in the spring, and Sarah your wife shall have a son." And Sarah was listening at the tent door behind him. Now Abraham and Sarah were old, advanced in age; it had ceased to be with Sarah after the manner of women. So Sarah laughed to herself, saying, "After I have grown old, and my husband is old, shall I have pleasure?" The LORD said to Abraham, "Why did Sarah laugh, and say, 'Shall I indeed bear a child, now that I am old?' Is anything too hard for the LORD? At the appointed time I will return to you, in the spring, and Sarah shall have a son." But Sarah denied, saying, "I did not laugh"; for she was afraid. He said, "No, but you did laugh" (Genesis 18:9-15).*

Here the first hint is given to Abraham as to who these guests are. They ask him, "Where is Sarah your wife?" Only the Lord could know of her recent name-change, but here is a man who asks, "Where is Sarah?" Abraham begins to realize then who this is, and when the question is followed with the repeated promise of a son, he is sure of the identify of his guest. Do you remember those two men on the Emmaus road, after the resurrection of our Lord, who did not recognize Jesus when he joined them? It was not until they saw him in the familiar act of breaking bread that they knew who he was. So when Abraham hears these familiar words about the promise of the son, he knows who it is that speaks.

Beyond the dividing curtain in the tent, Sarah has been listening. As she scrubs the pot just beyond the tent curtain she hears it all. She hears the question and the promise, and she realizes it is God who is saying she will have a son. She looks at her ninety-year-old body, long since almost dead. She looks in the mirror and sees the whiteness of her hair, the wrinkles in her face. She feels the arthritis in her bones. And when she hears this, she laughs cynically to herself.

We are told she made no sound at all, but laughed to herself. But beyond the curtain the Lord knew her thoughts and said to Abraham, "Why does Sarah laugh in her heart? Is anything too hard for the LORD? I'll set a date for this: I'll be back next spring and she shall have a son." And we read that Sarah was afraid. She saw that her heart was open and known to God. She saw that there was one who reads hearts as we read books, and she reacted just like we would. She denied she had laughed. But God knows that to justify or excuse our sin or to protect it and rationalize it and build a wall about it is to drive us into further misery and heartache. We cut ourselves off from divine help. And so the stern word comes to her. "No, but you did laugh. Admit it, face it: you did laugh, Sarah."

Remarkably enough, the account ends right here. Suddenly the subject is dropped, and another situation is introduced. We are left to wonder what this means. Back in chapter 17, when God announced to

Abraham for perhaps the fifth time that he was to
have a son, we are told that Abraham fell on his face
and laughed and said to himself, "Shall a child be
born to a man who is 100 years old? Shall Sarah who
is 90 years old bear a son?" This is a different kind of
a laugh than that of Sarah's. This is the laugh of
exulting joy over what God had promised. It is a
laughter of faith delighting in what God would do in
spite of the ravages of time and sin in his body. This
is what Paul refers to in Romans: "He did not weaken
in faith when he considered his own body, which was
as good as dead . . . " (Romans 4:19). Further, "No
distrust made him waver concerning the promise of
God, but he grew strong in his faith as he gave glory
to God, fully convinced that God was able to do what
he had promised" (Romans 4:20,21).

In contrast, Sarah's laughter is cynical, unbeliev-
ing. If this were the whole story we would be
tempted to say this woman is no example to follow.
But over in the New Testament, in the book of Hebrews, we get the rest of the picture. There in that
wonderful eleventh chapter, the hall of fame of the
heroes of faith, Sarah's name appears:

> By faith Sarah herself received power to conceive,
> even when she was past the age, since she considered
> him faithful who had promised (Hebrews 11:11).

Now we begin to see what must have happened.
After the guests left, Sarah was still thinking about
what she had heard, and the words of the Lord came
home to her heart in peculiar power—especially the
question God had asked, "Is there anything too hard
for the LORD?" As Sarah thought about it, she had to
face that question. Is there? Is anything too hard for
the LORD? She began to think of it—the Creator, the
one who called out of nothing the vast world in which

we live. She thought of what lay beyond, worlds without number that circle us in the limitless reaches of space. She thought of the one who sustains from day to day all the mighty, complex forces of earth, who brings the sun up on time, who guides the planets in their whirling courses, who predicts human events, and who centuries later brings them to pass exactly as he promised. Even the demons obey his word and tremble when they hear it.

As Sarah began to think of the one who had said these words, she felt the full force of that question, "Is anything too hard for the LORD?" As she began to look beyond the contrary facts of her own life and beyond the contrary feelings of her own heart, she said, "Of course not. Nothing is too hard for the LORD. If he has promised, then it shall be done." Through faith she received power to conceive when she was past age, because she counted him faithful who had promised.

What a beautiful lesson this is on the nature of faith! Faith looks beyond all the contrary circumstances to rest upon the character of the one who promised. Do not be misled by the popular delusion that faith stands by itself, that it is simply believing *anything*! Faith must have a promise to rest upon. Anything else is presumption, gullibility, folly. But when God has given a word, it is the word of God, and it can be trusted despite circumstance, feelings, or anything else. For is anything too hard for the LORD? Sarah rested upon that and believed God.

Does it seem hard to you to be what God wants you to be? Is it hard to crucify your evil nature? Hard to cast down evil imaginings and bring every thought into captivity to Christ? It is not too hard for the Lord! Does it seem hard to you to be made sweet and gracious and forgiving and loving when down inside you know how nasty and devious and unpleasant and perverse you can be? It is hard for you, but it is not too hard for the Lord! Does it seem hard that the friend for whom you are praying should ever be converted, or the one that is now rebelling against grace can ever be changed? Is anything too hard for the Lord? Does some task which God is now asking of you seem impossible? Some situation in which you are living—is it too hard and demanding for you? Well, it may be hard for you, but it is not too hard for the Lord. As faith learns to rest—not on its own inadequate resources but upon the unfailing resources of God in response to a definite promise—nothing is impossible.

> *Faith, mighty faith the promise sees,*
> *And looks to God alone.*
> *Laughs at impossibilities and cries,*
> *"It shall be done."*

When I was in Taiwan waiting to begin speaking at pastors' conferences, I confess I had a time of real fear and trembling. The night before the first conference we met at Tunghai University overlooking the city of Taichung. I was scheduled to begin my ministry in the morning. I attended the evening service and there were 300 or more pastors from up and down the length of the island, all speaking a different language from mine—all with a different cultural background. I knew that in the morning I would have to speak through two interpreters (anyone else would have needed only one, but I needed two), and that this would be a difficult barrier. I knew, too, that a whole summer's ministry of this kind stretched out before me. Here were three hundred men whom I'd never met before, to whom I was expected to minister.

Beyond that, in my mind's eye, I could see the conferences that were coming up in Vietnam, in Hong Kong, in Singapore, and in the Philippines. I was trembling and very uncertain. I felt the darkness and the oppressiveness of the pagan atmosphere in the land. I had already seen visible evidence of the power of darkness, the mark of the serpent throughout that island. So I went to the Lord in fear and trembling. I was reading through the Psalms at that time, and that night I came upon this word in Psalm 18. What a blessing it was!

> *Yea, thou dost light my lamp; the LORD my God lightens my darkness. Yea by thee I can crush a troop; and by my God I can leap over a wall (Psalm 18:28-29).*

I thought of the darkness of the land and of that group of 300 pastors, and that language barrier that stood between me and them. That was a wall over which I must leap, and there was a troop of 300 through which I must run. I laid hold of the promise of God that night and my heart was greatly lightened. The next morning God met us in a wonderful way, and I look back on that whole summer's ministry as one of the highlights of my life, seeing God at work throughout the difficulties, in spite of them, overcoming them.

If you want a wonderful experience, take your New Testament and use a concordance to look up the two little words, "but God." See how many times human resources have been brought to an utter end; despair has gripped the heart and pessimism and gloom has settled upon a people; and there is nothing that can be done. Then see how the Spirit of God writes in luminous letters, "But God," and the whole situation changes into victory. This is what God is offering to be and do in us and through us today. God responds the same way to us as he did to Abraham. When we are oppressed and confronted with circumstances beyond our ability to handle, we find the promise of God covers the situation. In prayer we can sense some prompting of the Spirit that gives us a word of faith to rest upon. Then, like Sarah, we may ask ourselves this question: "Is anything too hard for the LORD?" No, he is able to perform all that he says he will.

11
HOW PRAYER WORKS

(Genesis 18:16-33)

Beginning in the sixteenth verse of chapter 18 we read of three visitors coming out of the hot desert into Abraham's tent (who were unknown to him at first) who go their way to destroy Sodom and Gomorrah. Archaeologists are now convinced that the remnants of the ancient cities of wickedness—Sodom and Gomorrah—have been rediscovered lying under the waters of the Dead Sea. Our next chapter will take up the amazing historical event of their destruction; but now let us preview it.

Abraham accompanies his visitors as they leave his tent and go eastward to the valley of the Jordan. They come to a promontory at the edge of a steep ravine

which leads down to the Dead Sea, where they see the
doomed cities lying far below in the afternoon sun.
Tradition still marks this spot where Abraham inter-
vened with God for the city of Sodom.

We learn valuable lessons on the nature of prayer
in this section of Scripture. First, prayer begins with
the proposal of God:

> The LORD said, *"Shall I hide from Abraham
> what I am about to do, seeing that Abraham shall
> become a great and mighty nation, and all the na-
> tions of the earth shall bless themselves by him?
> No, for I have chosen him, that he may charge his
> children and his household after him to keep the
> way of the LORD by doing righteousness and jus-
> tice; so that the LORD may bring to Abraham
> what he has promised him." Then the LORD said,
> "Because the outcry against Sodom and Gomorrah
> is great and their sin is very grave, I will go down
> to see whether they have done altogether according
> to the outcry which has come to me; and if not, I
> will know" (Genesis 18:17-21).*

This marks a crucial fact concerning prayer: Prayer
never begins with man; it begins with God! True
prayer is never a man's plans brought to God for his
blessing. God is always the one who proposes. Prayer
begins when God enlists the partnership of man in
carrying out his program. Unless we base our prayers
on a promise, or a warning, or a conviction of God's
will, we have no right to pray.

Some people think the prayer of faith is crawling
out on a limb and then begging God to keep someone
from sawing it off. But that is not real prayer, that is
presumption. If God makes it clear that he wants you
out on a limb, fine—you will be perfectly safe there.
If not, it is presumptuous to crawl out on that limb,

expecting God to keep you there.

The difference is simply this: The prayer of faith is acting on previous knowledge of what God wants. It is always founded upon a promise. It begins with a proposal which God makes, or a conviction he gives, or a warning he utters. On the other hand, the prayer of presumption is to discover something we would like to do, and then asking God to bless it. That kind of thing is doomed at the outset. In fact, this is why so many "works of faith" fail, when they otherwise might have been wonderfully blessed.

When God proposes something, as he does here concerning the destruction of Sodom and Gomorrah, he usually enlists a man as his partner. We have here a picture of God talking to himself; he says, "Shall I hide from Abraham the thing I am about to do?" And he begins to list the reasons why he should include Abraham in his plan. Those reasons might be called, "the rights of friendship." Here is where Abraham earned the title which is given to him in both the Old and the New Testament, "the friend of God" (2 Chronicles 20:7; Isaiah 41:8; James 2:23).

God says, "I won't keep this from Abraham for two reasons: first, because by grace I have given him a favored position. He is the man whom I have called out to become great. Through him all the nations of the earth shall be blessed. Second, I have chosen him so that he might charge his household to keep the way of the LORD by doing righteousness and justice. I came into his life to show him how to do this. And because he has been taught by grace how to walk before God, this is the man to whom I will tell my secrets."

Do you see the parallel to the Christian today? Every believer in Jesus Christ stands in exactly the same relationship with God. We have been given by

grace—not through our own merits—a favored position before God. We have been called into the family
of God and made sons of the living God by faith in
Jesus Christ. Furthermore, we are being taught by
grace how to walk righteously before him. As we
learn that lesson, we become the people to whom
God tells his secrets. It is not enough to have the favored position. I think many Christians believe that
because they have accepted Jesus Christ, all God has
is now open to them. But there must be the walk, the
daily appropriation of what he is, so that we learn to
walk in righteousness. Only then does God begin to
share his secrets. Perhaps the reason some people get
more out of the Bible than others is that they have
learned this two-way relationship: God loves to tell
secrets to his obedient people.

God's proposal not only enlists the partnership of
man, but is based on an impartial and careful justice.
The Lord says to Abraham in verse 20:

> *Because the outcry against Sodom and Gomorrah*
> *is great and their sin is very grave, I will go down*
> *to see whether they have done altogether according*
> *to the outcry which has come to me.*

This, of course, is the language of accommoda-
tion. God does not need to go down and visit any city
in order to see what is going on. He is using
Abraham's own language to express the truth which
reflects his nature. He speaks as though a great outcry
has been coming to his throne from these wicked
cities. When I read this, I can't help but think that
every sin of man is like a voice crying out from earth
to heaven. What kind of a cry must be going up from
America today as a result of the terrible flood of por-
nography inundating our theaters and our literature?
God, according to this record, sees it all. God is

walking in our streets and taking note of all that happens to us. He visits our homes and marks everything, missing nothing. He invades our most sacred privacy. Even our thoughts are naked and open before him.

Before he judges the cities of the plain, God carefully investigates the charges, probing to see what the conditions are. Then he tells Abraham that he is going to destroy these cities. Actually, he does not specifically tell Abraham what he will do; but when Abraham hears the ominous words, "I will know," he realizes what God will do. Abraham knows all about the unbridled lust, the foul acts of homosexuality, the open passion for obscenity, the lurid and salacious attitude that permeated all public and private life in these cities. Abraham knows that the cities' doom is sure; this leads to the next step in prayer, the passions of man:

> So the men turned from there, and went toward Sodom {that is, the angels left and went on to the city}; but Abraham still stood before the LORD. Then Abraham drew near, and said, "Wilt thou indeed destroy the righteous with the wicked? Suppose there are fifty righteous within the city; wilt thou then destroy the place and not spare it for the fifty righteous who are in it? Far be it from thee to do such a thing, to slay the righteous with the wicked, so that the righteous fare as the wicked! Far be that from thee! Shall not the Judge of all the earth do right?" And the LORD said, "If I find at Sodom fifty righteous in the city, I will spare the whole place for their sake." Abraham answered, "Behold, I have taken upon myself to speak to the LORD, I who am but dust and ashes. Suppose five of the fifty righteous are lacking? Wilt thou

destroy the whole city for lack of five?" And he said, "I will not destroy it if I find forty-five there." Again he spoke to him, and said, "Suppose forty are found there." He answered, "For the sake of forty I will not do it." Then he said, "O let not the LORD be angry, and I will speak. Suppose thirty are found there." He answered, "I will not do it, if I find thirty there." He said, "Behold, I have taken upon myself to speak to the LORD. Suppose twenty are found there." He answered, "For the sake of twenty I will not destroy it." Then he said, "O let not the LORD be angry, and I will speak again but this once. Suppose ten are found there." He answered, "For the sake of ten I will not destroy it" (Genesis 18:22-32).

This is a remarkable account. It sounds as though Abraham is backing God into a corner and making him lower the ante every time. I wonder what we would have said if we had been in Abraham's shoes. I think some of us would have wrapped our robes of self-righteousness around us and said, "Good for you, LORD; they've got it coming. I wondered just how much you could take. I've long since had enough." Or perhaps we might have said, "LORD, do you mean you are going to destroy the city? All these wonderful people—I know they are evil, LORD, but they mean well. They have just been carried away a little bit. Don't be too hard on them." Perhaps we would have interceded in that way.

But Abraham had no time for self-righteousness, smugness, or sentimental nonsense. When these two angels left to go down to the city, this ordinarily would have been the cue for Abraham to say goodbye and get back to his tent. But it appears that Abraham did not let the LORD go. He stood yet before the

LORD. There was something on his heart, and we see in the following dialogue the emotion, the strong passion, that God's proposal awakened in this man's heart.

Several issues are of great interest in this account. First, Abraham recognizes the mercy of God. Notice that he says, "LORD, suppose there are fifty men in the city that are righteous. Wouldn't you spare the whole city for them?" Notice the way he is arguing. This is so easily misunderstood. Abraham is not trying to shame God into doing the right thing by appealing to his self-respect in this reminder: "Shall not the Judge of all the earth do right?" (Genesis 18:25b), as a mother might shame her child into doing right. God does not need anyone to remind him to do right, or to tell him it would be wrong to slay the righteous with the wicked. Rather, Abraham is basing his appeal on the knowledge of God's nature. He knows God would never destroy the righteous with the wicked. Now he is asking him to go further and spare the wicked for the sake of fifty righteous. Abraham thus reveals the basis of God's mercy in every age since then.

I remember a friend telling of walking past a church bulletin board one day and noting the announcement of the sermon: "If I were God." The man with my friend said, "'If I were God'"—that's an interesting title for a sermon. If I were God, I'd just lean down over the battlements of heaven, take a big, deep breath, and blow this earth out of existence." Why has not God done that long, long ago, with all the shameful record of human defiance, rebellion, and depravity which history records? It is because of this very principle to which Abraham appealed: There are righteous here.

The Lord said to his disciples, "You are the salt of

the earth" (Matthew 5:13a). The reason for salt is to preserve from corruption. A little bit of salt in meat will keep the whole thing from being destroyed or corrupted. This is why God permits human history to go on in its awful defiance; there are righteous on the earth—not men who are righteous in themselves, but who have been given the righteousness of Christ by faith in him. Our greatest defense against any satanic force lies not in any of our political scheming or maneuvering, but in the character of God who refuses to destroy the earth while there are righteous on it.

In addition to recognizing God's mercy, we note Abraham's awareness of his own state before God. In verse 27, Abraham answers: "Behold, I have taken upon myself to speak to the LORD, I who am but dust and ashes." LORD, I haven't any right to ask this of you. You, LORD, are wholly righteous and true, and I don't need to tell you what to do. Who am I, a man, talking to you—but LORD, I can't help but say this thing that is on my heart. Would you not spare the city if there are only 45 instead of 50?

This kind of language God delights to hear and honor, for it is the very opposite of the pride and deceit that makes us think we can demand of God what we want. I listened to a faith healer one day praying for people on the platform, and I was appalled at the way he spoke to God. He ordered him about as if God were a sort of magic genie obliged to do what this man ordered. It reflected the awful pride of his own heart. This is not true prayer. Abraham's approach is right: "LORD, who am I to speak to thee?"

The third consideration is for the protection of the righteous in Sodom. Abraham continues his dialogue until he comes down to ten people; then he stops there. Why does Abraham stop at ten? Perhaps because there were ten members in Lot's family. We learn in the next chapter that he and his own children and the ones they were to marry constituted exactly ten people. Abraham knew that, and he had Lot and his family in mind all along. He thought if he could just get the Lord to agree to save the city for ten, Lot's family would be saved—reasoning that by this time Lot must have won at least his own family to the Lord.

Abraham never asks God to spare Lot and his family, but out of compassion for the wicked, he keeps trying to save the whole city for the sake of Lot and his family. He appeals to God on whatever ground of mercy he can find. The evil of this city must often have revolted Abraham, this righteous man, but he is anxious to give it every last possible chance he can. The passion that speaks through true prayer is this recognition of God's mercy and the awareness of man's uncertain vision and limited wisdom. God is deeply concerned to protect the righteous. Simultaneously he is determined to have compassion on the foolish, lustful men who inflict the hurts. God seeks the slightest opening to show his mercy.

The purpose of prayer is suggested to us in verse 33: "And the LORD went his way, when he had finished speaking to Abraham; and Abraham returned to his place." It does not say, "and the LORD went his way when Abraham had finished speaking to him." It says, "when he had finished speaking to Abraham." Abraham did not quit here, God did. Some people say that Abraham's faith failed him when he got to ten. He did not dare try for anymore; but if he had, he would have saved the city of Sodom. I think that is highly unlikely. The next number he could have tried for would probably have been five, since he was diminishing the number by fives all

along. If he had asked for five that still would not
have saved the city. The next chapter tells us that
only *three* people got out of the city alive. *They were
the only righteous ones there.*

The verse suggests God initiated this whole conversation with Abraham. He led him along all
through it, and when Abraham had responded in
fullness as God desired, God ended the dialogue and
went his way. Abraham was not asking God to do
something for him; it was God who prayed in
Abraham and who set the limits of the conversation.
This agrees fully with what we read in the New Testament about prayer. In Romans Paul says, "For we
do not know how to pray as we ought" (Romans
8:26). Do you know what to pray for about yourself
or about anyone else? No, you don't. But he says the
Holy Spirit himself intercedes for us with groanings
which we cannot express, but which are nevertheless
there in the heart. True prayer, therefore, is never
merely man talking to God, but God talking to God
through man. It is God who causes Abraham to feel
his own compassion and to reflect his own desire for
an opportunity to show mercy. This is the reason for
prayer.

Admittedly, in talking about prayer, we are tread-
ing at the edge of mystery. But through the mists
certain things are clear from this account. Prayer
makes possible, first of all, the joy of partnership.
Did you ever see a little boy come into the house and
say to his mother, "I'm going to help daddy build the
house!" He is filled with pride about it, and he goes
out and passes up nails and holds the boards and
pounds his fingers. Daddy could have done the job
better by himself, but he loves to have his son help
him. And the son loves it, too. There is a sense of
partnership there. This is what prayer is. God seldom

moves all on his own. He loves to gather us in and have us help pound the nails. If we pound our fingers a bit, he is there to soothe us and to comfort us. This is why the apostle said we are called to be co-laborers with God, workers together with him. I read recently of a man who prayed, "Lord, break my heart with the things that break the heart of God." That is to hunger after this partnership with God.

Prayer also enables us to appropriate the character of God. Abraham is never more like God than at the moment he is praying for Sodom. His prayer did not save the city, and it was never intended to do so. But it did cause Abraham to reflect in his own life the mercy and compassion of God. This is why God asks us to pray, that we might take upon ourselves something of his own character. In that great verse about prayer in Philippians 4:6, Paul says, "Have no anxiety about anything, but in everything by prayer and supplication with thanksgiving let your requests be made known to God."

And what happens? Will God certainly do the thing you ask? No, that is not the promise. "And the peace of God, which passes all understanding . . . ." You cannot reason it out; you cannot explain it; no circumstance will permit you to understand the peace that rests at the heart of God and which will possess your hearts and minds. Circumstances may not be any different. You may rise from prayer and find your mother-in-law just as nasty as ever, your boss just as unreasonable, your children just as irritating, your husband just as stubborn, your wife just as bossy. Ah, but you have the peace of God that passes all understanding, keeping your heart and mind through any circumstance.

The third consideration: prayer focuses the power of God on an individual place or person. I don't understand this, but chapter 19, verse 29 says, "So it was that, when God destroyed the cities of the valley, God remembered Abraham, and sent Lot out of the midst of the overthrow." Lot received salvation, although Abraham had never mentioned Lot by name. God remembered Abraham and saved Lot. Now I don't know why prayer makes such a difference, but I know it does. You can plan a program, think through all the details, set up all the committees, get all the things you need, instruct everybody, rehearse it and run it through—and at the final presentation it may fall totally flat. But if you involve others in the ministry of prayer concerning it, though the preparations may be similar, the difference is that it comes with power, with impact, with full strength . . . and lives are changed.

One of our staff told us about a high school conference. Many of the young people said they hadn't planned to go, but something just made them go. When they got there, hearts which had been resisting the work of the Spirit—indifferent and letting things slide—were now open and listening, allowing the Lord to speak to them through the Word. They were changed— simply because all through the intervening weeks women had been gathering in homes and praying for that conference. I don't understand it, but I know it works. Prayer focuses the power of God.

The last principle here is that prayer affects the timing of God. Now this is a mysterious thing, but I am sure it is true. Certainly prayer does not change nor alter the will or purpose of God. Prayer is not a way to make God change his mind. When he announces something, he will do it. When he declares he will move in a certain direction, he always moves in that direction and no amount of prayer will ever change it. But prayer can defer judgment and it can also speed up blessing. It affects the timing. Have you ever noticed that time is one ingredient that God reserves for his own control? Jesus tells us plainly, "It is not for you to know times or seasons which the Father has fixed by his own authority" (Acts 1:6).

We have an example of how prayer affects God's timing in the case of Nineveh. When Jonah went there and announced "Yet forty days, and Nineveh shall be overthrown!", Jonah postponed the destruction of Nineveh. God waited almost one hundred years before he finally destroyed the city. Hezekiah in Judah had a severe illness, boils that were eating away his very life. God sent the prophet Isaiah to him to announce, "Fix up your house, you're going to die." At that word Hezekiah turned his face to the wall, wept and prayed, and said, "O God, spare my life." God heard, stopped Isaiah as he was going out the door, and told him to turn around and go back with another message. Isaiah went back in and said to the king, "God has heard your prayer and added fifteen years to your life." Prayer doesn't change God's purpose; but prayer does affect the timing.

There is a fascinating verse along this line which relates to our own lives today. Speaking about the problem of why God delays judgment, Peter says in his second epistle:

> The Lord is not slow about his promise as some count slowness, but is forbearing toward you, not wishing that any should perish, but that all should reach repentance. But the day of the Lord will come like a thief, and then the heavens will pass away with a loud noise, and the elements will be dissolved with fire, and the earth and the works that are upon it will be burned up (2 Peter 3:9,10).

Then he says these words:

> *Since all these things are thus to be dissolved, what sort of persons ought you to be in lives of holiness and godliness, waiting for and hastening the coming* of the day of God . . . (2 Peter 3:11).

If we are walking before the Lord as Abraham did and our hearts are available to God to pray through us and to reflect through us the passion that is in the heart of God, we can actually hasten the return of Jesus Christ to earth. We can hasten the day when the earth will be delivered from its oppressions and its burdens, when the golden age will break forth and righteousness will cover the earth.

12
THE WASTED YEARS

(Genesis 19)

The nineteenth chapter of Genesis is one of the most fascinating in the Word of God, and yet it is a grim and fateful story. The world has always had a morbid interest in the account of the destruction of Sodom and Gomorrah. Hollywood has seized upon this theme, making several films of it—it has everything they look for.

Science recently has taken a new interest in Sodom and Gomorrah. The discovery of ruins lying under the waters of the Dead Sea are thought by many experts to be the submerged remains of these wicked cities and the villages that clustered around them in the southern part of the Dead Sea plains. Rather than volcanic activity, some scientists have suggested that the cities were destroyed by lightning which set fire to the tar pits that saturated the area. That explanation would certainly serve this account in Genesis.

When we last looked at the life of Abraham, we found him moved by the Spirit to intercede for Lot in the city. The two angels that accompanied the Lord on his visit have gone on to destroy the cities, and Abraham and the Lord were left alone for that solemn exchange.

Now we pick up the story as the two angels come into Sodom in the evening hours. They enter looking like ordinary men—no wings or other identifying features. Although this chapter is rather long, there are really only two things to note about it. The first part gives us a view of Lot in the city of Sodom, while the rest of the chapter reveals how much of Sodom was in Lot.

First, we see Lot in Sodom:

> The two angels came to Sodom in the evening; and Lot was sitting in the gate of Sodom. When Lot saw them, he rose to meet them, and bowed himself with his face to the earth, and said, "My lords, turn aside, I pray you, to your servant's house and spend the night, and wash your feet; then you may rise up early and go on your way." They said, "No; we will spend the night in the street." But he urged them strongly; so they turned aside to him and entered his house; and he made them a feast, and baked unleavened bread, and they ate (Genesis 19:1-3).

The expression we find at the beginning of this account, "Lot was sitting in the gate of Sodom," is an eastern idiom which needs to be understood. This does not mean he was simply passing the time of day in the gate, watching strangers come into the city. This is a technical phrase which means he was the chief magistrate of the city of Sodom. His job was not only to give an official welcome to visitors of the city, but to investigate the nature of any strangers who might come, and also to administer justice concerning any quarrels within the city. The nearest equivalent we have today would be the office of mayor. So this account opens with the picture of Lot as the mayor of Sodom, the chief magistrate of the city.

This is interesting when we remember what we have already read of Lot. Here is the success story of the Old Testament, the familiar pattern of the immigrant boy from a foreign country who makes good in the big city. This is rags to riches, poverty to power, the country hick making good in the big town. You can imagine the biographies being circulated through the city, autographed personally by Lot.

We first met Lot when he left Ur of the Chaldees and moved to the city of Haran with Abraham. Although he was always subservient to Abraham, it seems very likely that Lot made a genuine response of faith to God on his own. When Abraham came into the land of Canaan, Lot went with him. When Abraham went down to Egypt, Lot went down with him. They came back wealthy men, although their time in Egypt was a period of great spiritual poverty and distress for both.

When they returned to Canaan, the first thing to happen was the quarrel between Lot's herdsmen and Abraham's herdsmen over pasture rights. Abraham, though he had the right of first choice as the elder, gave up his right to Lot. That significant choice was the beginning of Lot's downfall. He looked out and saw that the plain of Jordan was well-watered like the "garden of the LORD" and "the land of Egypt." It looked like both to him, and those two little phrases indicate the nature of Lot's choice. He had just come from Egypt, the place of materialism and commercialism—easy wealth—and this looked like such a place to him. And it looked like the garden of the LORD!

Now the garden of the LORD always indicates in the Scriptures a place of divine fellowship—as Adam and God walked together in the garden of Eden—the place where there was peace of heart and fellowship with God. Lot looked at the city of Sodom and the plain, and he thought this was the place where he could have both. He could make an easy living, advance himself, have all the cultural advantages of the city and still have fellowship with God. He wanted it all. So we read, "He chose for himself;" that is, he excluded everything but his own desire. On that basis, he arranged his priorities—to obtain wealth and to have fellowship with God.

In doing this, Lot disregarded the principle that runs all the way through Scripture and through human life. This is expressed by our Lord in the Sermon on the Mount when he says, "Seek first the kingdom of God and his righteousness" (Matthew 6:33). The promise that goes with that is that all these other material things will be added. But we are to "seek *first* the kingdom of God and his righteousness." Lot did exactly the opposite, placing materialism first. His first priority was to find a place where he could make a good living and advance his family's material advantages. With that, however, he wanted to have the kingdom of God and fellowship with him. We see the result as we follow the story.

At first Lot pitched his tent toward Sodom. He was not in the city, but he was near it. He was still in his tent; he was a sojourner in the land and the tent marked his pilgrim character. But he pitched it just outside the city of Sodom in order to take advantage of all the cultural pursuits of the city. Then in chapter 14 we find him dwelling in Sodom. By the time of the invasion of the five kings, he had moved right into the city. And now in chapter 19 we learn he is the mayor of the town.

Now I want to be fair with this man Lot; I believe he meant to do the right thing. It is clear from the whole story of his life that though he wanted to get something out of Sodom, he also expected to put something into Sodom. He probably thought to himself, "I may do these people good. I may be able to win some of them from evil to faith. I can make money faster here than anywhere else, that's true, but I also may help clean up the city a little. It's a wicked place, and perhaps I can improve its moral life." When Lot moved into Sodom, this is undoubtedly what he had in mind. But before long he becomes the mayor of the town, the most respected man in the city, the leader of its civic life. This is where the angels found him when they came into the city on that eventful evening.

I would like to ask this successful man four questions. I think they will reveal how much there is of Sodom in Lot, and how much the life of the city had affected him. The rest of the chapter will give us answers to these questions.

"Lot, you made a great success out of your life. You've won your way from a nobody to the mayor of the city. You entered as an unknown, a foreigner, and you've achieved both wealth and honor here in Sodom. My first question is this: How has your choice of life in Sodom affected your own inner life? You wanted both the personal advantages of the city life and fellowship with God; have you found it? My second question is this: How effective has your life been in changing the city's evils? The third question: How much money did you make there? How advantageous materially was it to live there? And my last question is, what influence did the city's life have on your own family?"

Now I think you will agree these are fair questions to ask a man who only wants to gain the best he can from the world and live a life of fellowship with God. The answers are all here in this chapter.

The first question is: "Lot, how about your own heart and mind in the midst of that city—what effect did Sodom have on your spiritual life?" Here are the answers:

> *But before they lay down {that is, the angel visitors}, the men of the city, the men of Sodom, both young and old, all the people to the last man, surrounded the house; and they called to Lot, "Where are the men who came to you tonight? Bring them out to us, that we may know them." Lot went out of the door to the men, shut the door after him, and said, "I beg you, my brothers, do not act so wickedly. Behold, I have two daughters who have not known man; let me bring them out to you, and do to them as you please; only do nothing to these men, for they have come under the shelter of my roof." But they said, "Stand back!" And they said, "This fellow came to sojourn, and he would play the judge! Now we will deal worse with you than with them." Then they pressed hard against the man Lot, and drew near to break the door. But the men put forth their hands and brought Lot into the house to them, and shut the door. And they struck with blindness the men who were at the door of the house, both small and great, so that they wearied themselves groping for the door (Genesis 19:4-11).*

Notice the extent of evil in this city. This is the reason God judged it. In verse 4 it says that *all* the men of the city both young and old, *all* the people to the last man surrounded the house. Though the language is veiled here in order to make possible a public discussion of the hideous sin, nevertheless, homosexuality is what all the people of Sodom were involved in. As you read this account you can see that Lot's reaction is disgust and shame. And this is no isolated instance; this was just a common, ordinary event in Sodom. In the second letter of Peter in the New Testament, we have Lot's reaction to life in Sodom:

> . . . *righteous Lot, greatly distressed by the licentiousness of the wicked (for by what that righteous man saw and heard as he lived among them, he was vexed in his righteous soul day after day with their lawless deeds) (2 Peter 2:7,8).*

That is a picture of discontent, of bafflement, of frustration. His soul was continuously vexed. He had tasted enough of the higher things of fellowship with God that he could never, never be satisfied with these sordid, ugly, obscene and lewd things of Sodom. Where is rest and peace and quietness of heart? It is up there with Abraham in his tent under the oak tree. But here in the city of Sodom is this man Lot. What good is it to have luxuries and wealth and every material gain if the heart is continually filled with a great distress that cannot be softened or satisfied? Lot's answer to that first question must be that his own life is grievously thwarted and blighted by the life of Sodom.

How about question two: Lot, what did you do for Sodom? When you moved into the city, you intended to influence the city, and you did; you became the

mayor, the chief magistrate. Now Lot, in that place
of great political influence, how many did you win?
How many did you turn from evil to faith? Again we
read:

> Then the {angels} said to Lot, "Have you any one
> else here? Sons-in-law, sons, daughters, or anyone
> you have in the city, bring them out of the place; for
> we are about to destroy this place, because the outcry
> against its people has become great before the
> LORD, and the LORD has sent us to destroy it." So
> Lot went out and said to his sons-in- law, who
> were to marry his daughters, "Up, get out of this
> place; for the LORD is about to destroy the city."
> But he seemed to his sons-in-law to be jesting
> (Genesis 19:12-14).

What a statement that is! With his very own sons-
in-law he had no influence whatsoever. When
Abraham had pleaded with God for divine mercy,
there needed to be found only ten righteous men in
this city for the whole city to be spared. But when
Lot went out beginning with his own family, he
could find none. His political power was great, but
his spiritual influence was absolutely nil.

Let us come to the meanest question of them all:
Lot, how much did you make while you were in
Sodom? What do you have to show for your years
there? Here is the record:

> When morning dawned, the angels urged Lot, say-
> ing, "Arise, take your wife and your two
> daughters who are here, lest you be consumed in the
> punishment of the city." But he lingered; so the men
> seized him and his wife and his two daughters by
> the hand, the LORD being merciful to him, and
> they brought him forth and set him outside the city.
> And when they had brought them forth, they said,

"Flee for your life; do not look back or stop anywhere in the valley; flee to the hills, lest you be consumed." And Lot said to them, "Oh, no, my lords; behold, your servant has found favor in your sight, and you have shown me great kindness in saving my life; but I cannot flee to the hills, lest the disaster overtake me, and I die. Behold, yonder city is near enough to flee to, and it is a little one. Let me escape there—is it not a little one?—and my life will be saved!" He said to him, "Behold, I grant you this favor also, that I will not overthrow the city of which you have spoken. Make haste, escape there; for I can do nothing till you arrive there." Therefore the name of the city was called Zoar {which means little}. The sun had risen on the earth when Lot came to Zoar.

Then the LORD rained on Sodom and Gomorrah brimstone and fire from the LORD out of heaven; and he overthrew those cities, and all the valley, and all the inhabitants of the cities, and what grew on the ground. But lot's wife behind him looked back, and she became a pillar of salt. And Abraham went early in the morning to the place where he had stood before the LORD; and he looked down toward Sodom and Gomorrah and toward all the land of the valley, and beheld, and lo, the smoke of the land went up like the smoke of a furnace. So it was that, when God destroyed the cities of the valley, God remembered Abraham, and sent Lot out of the midst of the overthrow, when he overthrew the cities in which Lot dwelt (Genesis 19:15-29).

If you want to know how much Lot made in Sodom, I suggest you make a trip to the Holy Land.

Go and stand by the shore of the Dead Sea and look out over that lifeless, brackish waste, the lowest and most desolate spot on the face of the earth, 1,300 feet below sea level. Listen to the lifeless waves lap the beach in an unending monotone of death. Nothing grows there, nothing lives, nothing moves in all that forsaken valley. How much did Lot win? He lost it all, everything. Here is the disastrous failure of this man. He was a good man who wanted to do right; but he chose his own way and lost his peace, his influence, and all that he had. *Still* he longs for a city, even a little one. The life of the city has so gripped his heart that he *must* have it.

The last and most terrible question is this: Lot, what about your family? When you turned your back on the tent and went to live in Sodom, what happened to your children? We have just seen how Lot lost his wife. Her heart was knit to the lusts and pleasures of the city, and she looked back. Doubtless she was caught by the flames and burned where she stood. Her body was then encrusted with salt as the debris-laden winds blew across her. She became just a pillar of salt as described here. The Lord Jesus recalled this incident in a solemn passage of warning, saying, "Remember Lot's wife" (Luke 17:32). And now we have this account of how the filthy way of the city had become part of his daughters' thinking. The dreadful story is recorded in verses 30-38:

> Now Lot went up out of Zoar, and dwelt in the hills with his two daughters, for he was afraid to dwell in Zoar; so he dwelt in a cave with his two daughters. And the first-born said to the younger, "Our father is old, and there is not a man on earth to come in to us after the manner of all the earth. Come, let us make our father drink wine, and we

*will lie with him, that we may preserve offspring
through our father." So they made their father
drink wine that night; and the first-born went in,
and lay with her father; he did not know when she
lay down or when she arose. And on the next day,
the first-born said to the younger, "Behold, I lay
last night with my father; let us make him drink
wine tonight also; then you go in and lie with him,
that we may preserve offspring through our
father." So they made their father drink wine that
night also; and the younger arose, and lay with
him; and he did not know when she lay down or
when she arose. Thus both the daughters of Lot
were with child by their father. The first-born bore
a son, and called his name Moab; he is the father
of the Moabites to this day. The younger also bore
a son, and called his name Ben-ammi; he is the
father of the Ammonites to this day.*

These two girls were virgins in body, but they
were already debauched in mind. They had long since
grown accustomed to obscenity and unrestrained
luridness, so up in the cave on the mountainside they
seized the thinnest tissue of excuses and the story
ends in a foul orgy of drunkenness and incest. Lot had
nothing but heartbreak and grief to show for the years
in Sodom. The Lord said, "for whoever would save
his life will lose it" (Matthew 16:25). So Lot, trying
to get the best out of both worlds, lost all and has
become for all time the picture of the Christian who
is saved, "but only as through fire" (1 Corinthians
3:15). He has nothing but wasted years to look back
on and eternity ahead.

I am sure you have seen many lessons in this story,
but let me press home just two of them. The first is
this: The hour of danger is when you first begin to

choose. Young people especially feel the pull to be like the world, wanting to be popular and to have what everyone else has, and do what everyone else does. They want to be welcomed by their crowd and to be Christians as well. They desire fellowship with Christ and a life of joy and power. Thus, many try to do exactly what Lot tried to do—compromise, so as to have both—and like Lot they have chosen for themselves, putting popularity and self first. Some young people, teenagers from Christian homes, are drinking, gambling, and stealing, then lying about it at home. They are playing with sex as far as they dare, and sometimes further. They do it because they want to be accepted and popular at school. At the same time they want also to be in church to find the Lord, have his blessing and fellowship.

Both life and the Scriptures teach that you cannot do both. No man can serve two masters. No one can walk down two diverging roads at the same time. If you are trying to live this way, if you have chosen your own desires first, you will surely lose it all, just as Lot did. Unless you change your mind and begin to actually put God first, before all else, you will continue in the very pattern that is traced out here. Then one day you will awaken to find it has all gone by. As Lord Byron wrote at the age of 29, after he had tried everything that life offered,

> *My days are in the yellow leaf;*
>   *The flower, the fruit, of life is gone.*
> *The worm, the canker, and the grief*
>   *Are mine alone!*

It is quite possible to fight your way to the top of the heap and then look back on a burned-out life, to see nothing but empty, wasted, barren years. The hour of choosing is *now*, in youth, when you are young, when you set your direction of life.

The second lesson is that when you attempt to gain the best of both worlds, you destroy others besides yourself. What was the greatest pang in Lot's heart when he awoke there in that cave in the mountains to learn all that had happened? Do you think it was grief over his lost wealth, his vanished honor, his troubled mind? Do you not think that the greatest, deepest wound of all in that man's heart was the recognition of what he had done to his loved ones in Sodom, his little girls, his wife?

You who are parents are being watched by your children. They see your outward respectability, your desire to be right and to do good. But they also see in some of you that the deepest thing in your life is to "get ahead" or to enjoy pleasure. They see that you will quickly sacrifice a prayer meeting for a night out, that you are always willing to take a bigger salary, regardless of what it may do to the family. They see that the things you sacrifice for and are willing to skimp and save for are not missions, or the church, or the work of God, but a new car or a color television set or nicer furniture or a longer vacation or a more pretentious home. They are watching and they see all this.

Bit by bit they lose interest in the Bible, Sunday School and church. They resolve to "get ahead" in the world and win the respect of Sodom no matter what moral restraint they have to abandon to do it. Often this is the tragedy of Christian homes where children are turning from God. And the sorrow you will carry to your grave, the deepest sorrow of your heart, will be that, though you still have your own faith, yet because of your compromise you have lost your children. This tragic story of Lot is taking place right here and now in the modern Sodom and Gomorrah in which we live.

But it does not have to be so! Yonder on the hill is Abraham, whose whole life principle was to let God choose and to be satisfied with that choice though it meant a tent all his days. His first question was never, "how much will I make," but, "will it destroy my tent and my altar? Those are the precious things in my life and I want nothing to do with anything which destroys my sense of pilgrimage, my sense of not belonging here, and my fellowship with the living God." In the end, Abraham gained the whole land—all that Lot possessed and more besides— and he shall inherit the earth, according to the Scriptures, for he looked for a city that has foundations, whose builder and maker is God.

abe looked
fwd to x-
we back.

13
OLD NATURES NEVER DIE

(Genesis 20)

Immediately following the destruction of Sodom and Gomorrah we are confronted with a lesson vital to the life of faith. We last saw Abraham on a promontory overlooking the Valley of the Dead Sea and interceding with God on behalf of the wicked cities of the plain. This is a highpoint in Abraham's life, when he seems to have grown to a position of tremendous power, authority, and friendship with God. This is what many Christians expect in their lives. They have the idea that as forgiven sinners they will gradually learn to improve themselves until they become at last worthy of Christ's friendship and can enter into the secrets of God in some amazing way as Abraham did here.

But this idea of the Christian life, as this story reveals, is *wrong*. The account which continues in chapter 20 might be entitled, "Relapse." Doesn't it sound familiar?

> *From there Abraham journeyed toward the territory of the Negeb, and dwelt between Kadesh and Shur; and he sojourned in Gerar. And Abraham said of Sarah his wife, "She is my sister." And Abimelech king of Gerar sent and took Sarah.*

Here is Abraham doing the same thing he had done thirty years before. He is down in the land of Gerar, the sea coast country on the southwest side of Palestine, just above the Gulf of Suez on the way to Egypt. The people who lived in this area were later called Philistines. These were the enemies of Israel from whom came Goliath, the giant David slew. These people had come from Egypt. They were not Canaanites, but Egyptians who had moved up to the border of the land of Palestine. They are a spiritual picture of the moral but unregenerate churchman; that is, a worldly people getting as close to the truth of God as they can while remaining unregenerate.

The world is full of these religious people. Thousands of them meet in churches across our land who do not know what it means to be born again. They do not know what it is to have the life of Christ dwelling in them. They think the church is where they can learn ethical and moral principles along with others who are interested in advancing the highest good of society. Yet they consider themselves Christians and would feel insulted if they were told that they are not Christian in the scriptural sense.

The king of this group is called Abimelech, which means "my father is king." This suggests an authority no higher than man; it is the concept of "my father as king of all the people," the supreme ruler. This is characteristic of the worldly church, the church that *man has ⊖ in him* does not regard authority as coming from any higher source than man. These are the Philistines—"holding the form of religion but denying the power of it" (2 Timothy 3:5).

These are the people among whom Abraham walks. He is evidently upset by what had happened in the destruction of the cities of the plains, and perhaps longs to get away from that infamy and terror. So he moves down into the south country and comes among these people. The first thing he does there is to tell a lie about his wife. He says she is his sister, exactly as he did 30 years before. This woman Sarah is still such a lovely creature that she is a lure to *Knockout* all the wolves around, and Abraham feels the only way to protect himself is to say that she is his sister. Just as before, the king comes and takes her as his own . . . and Abraham is in trouble.

> *But God came to Abimelech in a dream by night, and said to him, "Behold, you are a dead man, because of the woman whom you have taken; for she is a man's wife." {That would not frighten anyone today, but it did then.} Now Abimelech had not approached her; so he said, "Lord, wilt thou slay an innocent people? Did he not himself say to me, 'She is my sister'? And she herself said, 'He is my brother.' In the integrity of my heart and the innocence of my hands I have done this." Then God said to him in the dream, "Yes, I know that you have done this in the integrity of your heart, and it was I who kept you from sinning against me; therefore I did not let you touch her. Now then restore the man's wife; for he is a prophet, and he will pray for you, and you shall live. But if you do not restore her, know that you shall surely die, you, and all that are yours (Genesis 20:3-7).*

Here is a picture of the blundering blindness of unbelief. This man is on the verge of committing a very
grievous sin when God stops him. This reveals how
God views this sin of taking another man's wife. He
tells this pagan man he is doing a terrible thing and
Abimelech recognizes it. You can see how far we have
slipped today, when you realize that even pagans of
that day recognized how terrible it was to take
another man's wife.

Abimelech protested that he did not realize what
he was doing, that he had been tricked, that he was
innocent of any wrongdoing and was acting only out
of his integrity. Notice, however, that his moral
standards were no protection against stumbling into
sin. Even though he had higher moral standards than
Abraham, they were no protection against keeping
him from wrongdoing. Even with his eyes wide open
and meaning to do right, and thinking he was doing
right, he was still on the verge of falling. This is the
unhappy state of all those who do not know Jesus
Christ as Lord. They do not have the inner voice to
protect, restrain, guide and keep them from evil.
Had it not been for the influence of God, this man
would have plunged right on into sin. For Abraham's
sake, God restrained him. And as we see at the end of
this account, he struck Abimelech with a deadly dis-
ease which prevented him from taking Sarah as his
wife. Undoubtedly this man thought a terrible
tragedy had occurred, but it was really the kindness
of God keeping him from something far more serious.

I wonder sometimes if many of the events that appear tragic are not the kind-heartedness of God,
keeping those who love him from evil. Paul writes of
one who restrains the full measure of human sin.
Even in his day, "The mystery of lawlessness is al-

ready at work" (2 Thessalonians 2:7a); but he says there is one "who now restrains it," keeping it in bounds. If God was not at work restraining human evil, man would long since have blown himself off the face of the earth. He has never needed atom bombs or hydrogen warheads to do the job. They only speed up the process. He could have done it long, long ago by simpler means— axes, hatchets, knives and swords would have done the trick—and he would have done so if it had not been for God's restraining hand. Paul says the day is coming when God will take that restraint away, and all hell will break loose on earth. That cataclysm is vividly described for us in the Book of Revelation.

In the next section we find Abraham suffering from the reproach of Abimelech:

> So Abimelech rose early in the morning, and called all his servants, and told them all these things; and the men were very much afraid. Then Abimelech called Abraham, and said to him, "What have you done to us? And how have I sinned against you, that you have brought on me and my kingdom a great sin? You have done to me things that ought not to be done." And Abimelech said to Abraham, "What were you thinking of, that you did this thing?" Abraham said, "I did it because I thought, 'There is no fear of God at all in this place, and they will kill me because of my wife.' Besides, she is indeed my sister, the daughter of my father but not the daughter of my mother; and she became my wife. And when God caused me to wander from my father's house, I said to her, 'This is the kindness you must do me: at every place to which we come, say of me, "He is my brother." ' "
> (Genesis 20:8-13).

As a Christian has anyone had to say to you, "What were you thinking of when you did this thing?" Have you ever had to say it to yourself? "What got into me anyway? I thought I was further along in the Christian life than this. Here I have done this thing that I thought had long ago passed out of my life. Whatever got into me?" If you have ever had to ask yourself that, you need to learn the lesson Abraham had to learn here.

Old natures never die; they only smell that way! You are still capable of the worst sin that you have ever committed—and more. Abraham has been a coward for thirty years and he is still capable of the same yellow streak he had at the beginning—hiding behind his wife, subjecting her to dishonor and disgrace and shame in order to protect his own skin. He had made a pact with her thirty years before and he had never gotten around to giving her any new instructions in spite of how much he had grown in grace.

This old Adamic nature—with which we are born and which is so perverted and twisted that it never operates as God intended it to—is totally depraved. That does not mean it cannot do what appear to be nice things. There is something about the old self, the flesh, which is able to simulate righteousness. But even if the flesh succeeds in an outward show of a sweet and lovely nature, it has never achieved anything but self-righteousness. Self-righteousness always demands self-praise, a longing to be admired and to win the attention of others. If self-righteousness succeeds, it makes you an extrovert. If you fail in your pursuit of self-righteousness, the result is self-pity, and self-pity makes you an introvert. Either way it is the flesh, the same ugly thing. In neither case can it ever please God.

This is why when God comes into the human heart through Jesus Christ, he never tries to do anything about cleaning up that old nature. He writes it off as worthless. He says everything that comes from self is worthless. No matter how it looks in the eyes of others, if it comes from the self-advancing, self-centered core, it is worthless and it always will be. What you now are in the flesh, you always will be, if you live a hundred years.

Now isn't that encouraging? I hope it is. If you lay hold of that concept, you will find it one of the most encouraging truths in your Christian life. It will release you from that awful burden of self-effort which tries to make the old nature behave itself. You must renounce self, quit feeding it or protecting it or polishing it up or trying to make it look good. Give it up! Accept all that Jesus Christ is in you and wants to be through you, for his nature is perfect. If you will let him be what he wants to be through you, you will always be pleasing to God.

Any dependence upon self always results in the kind of experience that Abraham had. After thirty years of walking with God and learning wonderful lessons in the spiritual life, the minute he steps out of dependence upon God he steps back into that same ugly nature he had in the beginning—and it is unchanged after thirty years. Only by walking in the Spirit can old natures be kept out of the place of control. "Walk by the Spirit, and do not gratify the desires of the flesh," Paul tells us.

Let us suppose my family decided to prove that the popular conception about pigs—that a pig likes mud—is a complete insult to the nature of a pig. We are going to vindicate the pig by showing how it can be trained and educated to be what it is not by nature. We go get a little, silky, baby pig and bring it home.

I introduce this little pig to my children. We'll call it Flash. I tell them Flash is to be their baby brother and they are never to treat him in any way that would let him know he isn't human. If we treat him as human, he will be human.

So we begin Flash's training. We housebreak him, we teach him to wipe his feet when he comes to the door, to sit up at the table with a bib around his neck. We dress him in a little pink shirt with blue velvet pants, we tie a little bow around his tail, we teach him to stand up when a lady comes into the room and to be very mannerly. At first we make great progress. It seems as though we are succeeding because Flash is becoming very cultured and refined. But one day we make a serious and fatal mistake. We leave the door open.

The little pig takes one sniff of the spring air wafting in; and suddenly, like a bullet, Flash is out the door and heading for the biggest, dirtiest mud puddle he can find. As he scoots in and buries himself in the mud, he rolls over and over in uncontrolled glee, kicking his feet up and singing at the top of his piggy voice, "Be it ever so humble, there's no place like home."

No matter how you train it and no matter how you teach it, a pig is pig and mud puddles are home sweet home. You cannot break that nature. This is what Abraham demonstrates.

Let us now look at the last section:

> *Then Abimelech took sheep and oxen, and male and female slaves, and gave them to Abraham, and restored Sarah his wife to him. And Abimelech said, "Behold, my land is before you; dwell where it pleases you." To Sarah he said, "Behold, I have given you a thousand pieces of*

silver; it is your vindication in the eyes of all who are with you; and before every one you are righted." Then Abraham prayed to God; and God healed Abimelech, and also healed his wife and female slaves so that they bore children. For the LORD *had closed all the wombs of the house of Abimelech because of Sarah, Abraham's wife (Genesis 20:14-18).*

God healed Abimelech and blessed Abraham. This very last scene points up the difference between a Christian and a moral non-Christian. Abimelech was really more noble in this incident than Abraham, which means that Abimelech's old Adamic nature was more pleasant than Abraham's old nature. But both were a total failure in pleasing God. Perhaps you have noticed this difference. Some non-Christians can be more cultured, refined, and pleasant to live with than some Christians. The Christian who is living in his old nature in the energy of the flesh is quarrelsome, irritable, self-centered, and difficult to live with. But neither of them can please God with the old nature. Abraham had something which Abimelech didn't. He had a life from God, a regenerate heart, a new nature, so that when he repented, he was forgiven. God turned his failure into fullness and blessed him and caused him to be the instrument through which Abimelech was forgiven and restored. It was only when Abraham prayed for Abimelech that Abimelech was healed.

Do you see the distinction? What a lesson is here concerning the grace of God! When we slip back into the flesh and do some evil thing, we say, "I never seem to learn, it's the old nature again. I have slipped out of dependence upon Christ, and here I am back in this thing." But then we can come back to God and

tell him, "Lord, I don't know when I'll learn to rest
and depend upon you, and quit trying to make something out of this old nature. I've done it again. Now
take the mess, Lord, and straighten it out."

Remember when our Lord was in the garden of
Gethsemane? Temple soldiers and priests came to
take him by force, and Peter impetuously grabbed a
sword and struck off the ear of the high priest's servant. The Lord reached down, picked up the ear, and
replaced it (see John 18:10; Luke 22:51). I have often
thought this well describes what we so often do—we
go around lopping off people's ears. And the Lord is
so gracious to come along and put it back on, heal it,
and give us a place of blessing as he did with
Abraham. He corrects our mistakes and turns the
very failures of our life into fullness, the very obstacles into opportunity, the stumbling blocks into
stepping stones to further blessing for the grace of
God.

This is a lesson we must learn. We have not been
called to improve ourselves, but to quit trying to improve ourselves and to recognize what we are. In ourselves we can never be good enough; we must appropriate all that Christ can be to us and through us.
Only his life is satisfying to God. His life is acceptable, his life is perfect, his life is the life of peace, joy,
blessing. His is a life of compassion, truth, honesty,
and sincerity. As we allow him to live that life anew
through us, we will demonstrate the same character-
istics of grace, blessing and fullness that he does.

14
ISHMAEL MUST GO!

(Genesis 21:1-14)

Our new life in Christ begins with an initial period of joy and gladness, frequently with fruitful activity and many observable changes. I always question the conversion of someone who doesn't soon show some changes in his life, because the very purpose for which Christ enters our life is to redeem us, to buy us back out of uselessness into usefulness. This initial period is almost always one of great joy. We recognize that we have found the secret of life, that all the empty cisterns from which we have been trying to satisfy our thirsty soul are no longer of any avail, so we turn to the fountain of living water. The result is always an experience of genuine gladness in the soul (varying to some degree with the personality involved).

Our conversion is almost always followed by a period of failure and frustration, alternating with times of peace and joy and victory. This is a problem for many young Christians. They believe they are going to continue in that initial level of gladness, triumph, and victory, and are very disturbed at first when failure, frustration and defeat come into their lives. But they struggle on through that and come into a time of renewed peace and victory, only to fail again. This sometimes goes on for years and years. It doesn't need to go on that long, but it often does.

Many waste years trying to recapture the first love they had and the joy they first experienced when they came to Christ. But this is a mistake, and Christians need to realize that these periods of frustration and failure are part of the divine plan of God. When we fail to see that, we become like those Galatians to whom Paul wrote saying, "Oh, foolish Galatians! Who has bewitched you, before whose eyes Jesus Christ was publicly portrayed as crucified?" (Galatians 3:1). Are you really able to work this out in your own strength, having begun in the power of another? Thus he corrects them, and this is what we need, too, to learn. The periods of failure are simply designed to teach us how to live the new way of life.

We have two centers of being from which we can operate: what we were in ourselves, and what we are now in Christ. Whenever we operate from self we fail. Whenever we depend upon Christ we triumph. The Lord simply lets us experience both until we finally learn the difference. We are not to depend upon self! Victory comes only through total dependence on Christ and him alone. As we gradually learn this, there are increasingly frequent times of victory, peace, joy, effectiveness, and fruitfulness in our life, and there comes at last the long- promised era of continuous fruitfulness. One morning we take a good look at our lives and notice what is happening. That nature, that disposition we have long been trying to achieve— love, joy, peace, gentleness, goodness, patience, meekness, and self-control—is beginning to appear more and more in our life. That first long-promised joy has begun to be fulfilled.

This is the place to which we come in the life of Abraham. At the beginning God promised him a son who would bring joy to his heart. This son would begin a long line of descendants that eventually would outnumber the stars in the sky. But the promised joy was long delayed. Abraham went though many trials and failures in which he learned much about himself through both defeat and folly. And when the victories and fulfillments came, he learned much about God.

By now he has begun to walk so consistently in the Spirit that the continual fruit of love, joy, and peace begin to appear. This is what the birth of Isaac symbolizes here; when Isaac is born, Abraham's joy is fulfilled.

> *The LORD visited Sarah as he had said, and the LORD did to Sarah as he had promised. And Sarah conceived, and bore Abraham a son in his old age at the time of which God had spoken to him. Abraham called the name of his son who was born to him, whom Sarah bore him, Isaac. And Abraham circumcised his son Isaac when he was eight days old, as God had commanded him. Abraham was a hundred years old when his son Isaac was born to him. And Sarah said, "God has made laughter for me; every one who hears will*

laugh over me." And she said, "Who would have
said to Abraham that Sarah would suckle chil-
dren? Yet I have borne him a son in his old age"
(Genesis 21:1-7).

This is the joy of fulfillment. At last we have two
sons of Abraham living side by side, Isaac and
Ishmael. We don't need to wonder what this means
in the life of faith, because Paul tells us in the letter
to the Galatians. He says that Isaac pictures that
which is born of the Spirit, while Ishmael is a picture
of that born of the flesh (Galatians 4:28). Isaac is the
result of a life controlled by the Spirit. What does
that mean to us? Well, in that same letter he tells us,
"the fruit of the Spirit is love, joy, peace, patience,
kindness, goodness, faithfulness, gentleness, self-
control" (Galatians 5:22). These are the Isaacs for
which we have been waiting. Ishmael, on the other
hand, stands for the works of the flesh outlined in
that very same chapter.

Notice how that is confirmed in this passage.
First, Isaac's birth was *supernatural*. He was not born
until Abraham and Sarah had reached an advanced
age. Sarah was 90 years old and Abraham was 100. It
occurred at a set time, some 30 years after God had
first promised to give Abraham a son. In Romans
4:19, Paul refers to this when he says, "He did not
weaken in faith when he considered his own body,
which was as good as dead because he was about a
hundred years old." This was a supernatural birth.
God restored the natural processes and a child was
born. Amazing, isn't it?

Do you see now why God waited all this long time
to fulfill the promise to Abraham? He was waiting
until the ability and forces of natural man had failed,
so his promise could only be fulfilled supernaturally.

This is exactly what God says to us about the fruit of the Spirit in our lives. It will never come from the flesh. It will never come from self-effort nor by positive thinking nor by perpetual trying. Love, joy, and peace, those wonderful gifts of God, never come from any attempt on our part. You can imitate them, but they will never be anything but a poor imitation. You cannot produce the fruit of the spirit by the flesh, for that fruit is a supernatural gift from the life lived in the power of the Spirit of God, born as Isaac was here. It comes simply by appropriating the life of Jesus Christ.

The second principle about this new life is circumcision. Abraham set upon Isaac the sign of God's ownership, which pictures what the Christian does when he recognizes that the love, joy, and peace in his heart is not given for his own private enjoyment, but to share with others. God doesn't make you easier to live with simply to clear up some of the problems in your home, but to demonstrate through your life the transforming grace of Jesus Christ. You are to use it to bless others.

When I was a boy in Minnesota, we had a neighbor with a large family who was regarded as a religious fanatic. We'd hear stories about how she would take her Bible and go out into the fields and spend all day in a haystack. But to do it she neglected her own household. Her children were always running around without proper direction in very dirty clothes, her house was always filthy, and her husband was always complaining. Nevertheless, she would come to church, stand up, and testify about what a wonderful experience she had had out in the haystack and what joy and ecstasy had come into her heart. She may well have had those experiences; we have to take people at their word in this respect. But it was an

uncircumcised joy and love. It was not devoted to the
purpose for which God had sent it. It did not bear the
mark of God's ownership. It wasn't used in the way
God intended it to be used. But when Isaac is born in
Abraham's household, he is circumcised to portray
the truly dedicated life.

The third principle in this account is the reality of
satisfaction. Isaac means laughter, and when this son
was born the whole household was beside itself with
ecstasy. I wish we could have seen Sarah, ninety years
old, with that little babe in her arms, her face radiant
with delight in the long-awaited fulfillment of the
desire of her heart. What a picture this is of the joy
that Christ brings into the human heart! All language is inadequate. The song writer has said:

> *Heaven above is softer blue, earth around is sweeter*
> *green, Something lives in every hue, Christless eyes*
> *have never seen,*
> *Birds with gladder songs o'er flow, Flowers with*
> *deeper beauties shine Since I know as now I know,*
> *I am his and he is mine*

This is the experience of those who have Christ
dwelling in their hearts. Have you ever had an Isaac
experience, when after a long period of struggle you
discovered the secret of walking in the Spirit, and the
fruit of the Spirit blossomed in your life? What a day
of glad release this is when you have put away all the
self-centeredness and begin to bear that wonderful
fruit of Christ-centered love, joy, and peace!

But this is not the whole story. A sharp contrast
appears in the next section:

> *And the child grew, and was weaned; and*
> *Abraham made a great feast on the day that Isaac*
> *was weaned. But Sarah saw the son of Hagar the*

Egyptian, whom she had borne to Abraham, play-
ing with her son Isaac. So she said to Abraham,
"Cast out this slave woman with her son; for the
son of this slave woman shall not be heir with my
son Isaac." And the thing was very displeasing to
Abraham on account of his son. But God said to
Abraham, "Be not displeased because of the lad
and because of your slave woman; whatever Sarah
says to you, do as she tells you, for through Isaac
shall your descendants be named. And I will make
a nation of the son of the slave woman also, because
he is your offspring." So Abraham rose early in the
morning, and took bread and a skin of water, and
gave it to Hagar, putting it on her shoulder, along
with the child, and sent her away. And she de-
parted, and wandered in the wilderness of
Beersheba (Genesis 21:8- 14).

Now if Isaac represents the fullness of the fruit of
the Spirit, then Ishmael represents some pet sin of
our self-life in which we find comfort and delight and
which we do not want to surrender. You see how perfectly this is reflected here in this story—some value
which we have long suspected is not God's choice,
but which we are reluctant to give up. Perhaps it is
some long-standing habit such as smoking or overeating. I am not making any lists of forbidden things;
I am merely saying we can protect habits or values
which are really some form of self- indulgence. God
may allow them for awhile, but the time comes when
he says, "These have to go."

It can be anything. It may be some pet doctrine
which has been dividing and separating the brethren.
You've gained a reputation in this field as an authority and you are not going to give it up. Maybe you
insist on a particular mode of baptism, a matter of

tithing, some partisan political view—something that separates but which you hold as distinctive. It may be some friendship or membership in some lodge or club. It can be anything that rises from self-indulgence which we defend, protect, justify and delight in, just as Abraham defended, protected and delighted in Ishmael—until the time came when he had to make this choice.

Notice some things about this. First of all, this distressed Abraham. He had to go through an agonizing reappraisal when the word came from the Lord, "Ishmael must go." He loved this boy—though he had often grieved over his arrogance and hasty ways—and he didn't want to give him up. I think he was angry with God for bringing the matter up. He probably said to God, as we frequently say, "Oh, this is really nothing, it is such a trivial thing. Why bring it up, why bother with it? Let's go on the way we were. We have been getting along for quite awhile with Ishmael—why change now?" But the agony of his heart showed that it was not trivial. If it had been a light matter, he could easily have dismissed Ishmael. But it was not; it was something that would cost him deeply.

I remember a telephone call from a lady who had attended a class I taught. She said, "I've been thinking so much about what you said in class about God asking us to turn away from things in our life that are hindering us. I have a problem, and I don't know what to do about it." She named what it was, and she said she had heard testimonies from people about what God had done for them when they became Christians and how they had had problems with smoking or drinking or sex or some other habit that God had laid it on their hearts to stop.

She said, "They tell me God just takes the desire away and they don't ever have the desire to do it again. I know that God would have me turn from this particular problem in my life, but he doesn't take the desire away. What should I do?"

I said to her, "Well, God does sometimes deliver us by taking the desire out of our hearts; but in most cases, I think, God leaves the desire right there and tells us to obey anyhow— even though it costs us some heartache and anguish." I quoted this story of Abraham to her, of how he obeyed when it hurt, when it caused anguish to his heart to say goodbye to Ishmael. But because God said this thing was harming him, he obeyed God and sent his son away.

I want you to notice that this was a delayed judgment. Ishmael was fourteen years old at this time, and Abraham had known from the beginning that Ishmael was not God's choice. He had come from Abraham's deliberate, self-indulgent choice. Since God had not chosen this boy he would not be Abraham's heir. Yet God permitted him to stay, saying nothing to Abraham about it until Isaac came along.

When we come to choices like this and the Spirit of the Lord speaks to us about a matter, we tend to think God is very harsh, very cruel, and very demanding—when in reality he has been patient, forbearing, and tender. For fourteen years Ishmael was allowed to stay in the house without a word; but when Isaac came, then Ishmael had to go at last. He never takes away an "Ishmael" until he has given an "Isaac"! Because this is so, we need to be very careful about judging others. We may see Ishmaels in their lives and want to root them out, saying, "You must get rid of this habit." But when God takes away an

Ishmael, he first gives an Isaac. In other words, he never tells us to give up some self-indulgence until he has first given us some fruit of the Spirit of grace to take its place to satisfy that longing of the heart. But when he does give us that gift of grace and blessing, then the self-indulgence has to go.

When we first become Christians, there are some obviously evil things in our lives that have to go immediately. But there are others that appear more innocent which God permits to linger, allowing us to struggle and fight until we learn to walk in the Spirit. Then the fruit of the Spirit begins to appear and these things have to go.

A friend of mine told me about a prominent evangelical leader who had been given a great opportunity. He was looking forward to its fulfillment as the greatest joy he had ever known. Others had been praying for this man for a long time because they saw some Ishmaels in his life. One day, as he was looking forward to moving in on this opportunity, a friend sat down with him and in a painful time faced him with some of the things in his life. It was the voice of God to him. The friend told him he was trying to be a big shot, always wanting to run things himself. He had to learn to let others step in. He put his finger on a personal habit, a bad temper, and told him that the next time he displayed that temper (as he had recently been doing) he would find his opportunity gone. He just laid it on the line with him and said, "Now that this opportunity has come, these things must go." This man, relating the incident to someone else, said, "I realized that this was the Spirit of God speaking to me." And he responded to it and faced the things, recognizing that they must go. This is always distressing; but it also represents the faithfulness and patience of God, who has allowed this Ishmael until we are ready to give it up.

Notice the last part—it is *decisive*. When God speaks, there can be no dilly-dallying. It is imperative that Ishmael goes. This is what our Lord Jesus spoke about in the Sermon on the Mount when he said, "If your right eye causes you to sin, pluck it out and throw it away . . . and if your right hand causes you to sin, cut it off and throw it away" (Matthew 5:29,30). If you are going to walk in the power of the Spirit, you cannot walk in the power of the flesh. You cannot have both; one must go.

Now, observe the following. God says definitely that Ishmael could never share in the inheritance with Isaac. This is exactly what Jesus meant when he said, "that which is born of the flesh is flesh, and that which is born of the Spirit is spirit" (John 3:6). When the time comes for us to stand before our Lord at the judgment seat of Christ, our lives will be classified into two areas: Those that are wood, hay, and stubble, which are of the flesh; and those of gold, silver and precious stones, which are of the Spirit (see 1 Corinthians 3:10-15). The Lord says to us, as he said to Abraham, "Ishmael must go." If you refuse to expose, to examine and remove that which is born of the flesh— even though you know God has said that it hurts you, and even though he has shown you the peace, joy, and love which is the fruit of the Spirit— then you must face this choice as Abraham did. *Ishmael must go* .

I recall reading an article about Dr. Donald Barnhouse and was struck by evidences of this very choice in his life. He said, "Early in my ministry I had the idea that I must strike out against all error wherever I saw it. I'd hit Christian Science, Unitarianism,

Romanism, and if error was in some fundamental leader with whom I was in ninety-five percent agreement, I swung hard at the five percent." This made Dr. Barnhouse a highly controversial figure, often unmercifully sharp and dogmatic. This zeal for truth within him became an Ishmael in his life.

Then he tells how there came a time when the Spirit of God taught him to love. Now he faced the choice—Ishmael had to go. He had to learn to be more understanding and more tolerant of others' variant views. He wrote, "Some time ago, I published a New Year's resolution expressing regret that I had had differences with men who are truly born again. The results of that resolution were astounding. In the years which followed its publication, my ministry has been transformed. I need to know all who have been redeemed by Christ, for I will never know my Lord fully until I see him in every individual life whom he has redeemed and saved by the outpouring of his life for us all upon the cross. This," he says, "is true fellowship." It was wonderful to see in the life of Dr. Barnhouse the removal of an Ishmael. The closing years of his life show much of the mellowing and sweetness of the fruit of the Spirit in one who before had been somewhat harsh, critical, and demanding.

I don't know what form Ishmael may be taking in your life, but I know there are times when God says to us, simply, "this must go; no longer may it be permitted." There can be nothing of the life of the Spirit until this is dealt with.

You know how Abraham obeyed. Early in the morning he got up, took bread and a skin of water— and though it cost him heartbreak to do it—sent Hagar and Ishmael out, so that he might have the fullness of the Spirit of life in Christ Jesus.

The Lord sees hurtful things in us of which we are not even aware. We protect, defend, excuse, justify, and try to find all kinds of ways to permit them to continue; but we can thank God that there comes a time when, in faithfulness, he says to us, "This must go. Cast out the bond woman and her son, for it is a threat to the inheritance and cannot have any part in it." If we would sincerely and earnestly long to be a full and completely yielded vessel of God's joy and strength and peace among men, we will cast out Ishmael—and with it find the fullness and joy of Isaac.

15
THIS THIRSTY WORLD

(Genesis 21:14-34)

As we trace through the *Pilgrim's Progress* of the Old Testament—the way God calls us from sinful rebellion to the land of fellowship with Christ—we now turn to chapter 21 of Genesis. All that took place in Abraham's life wonderfully pictures what happens in our own spiritual progress. When Abraham obeyed God's call and came into the land of Canaan, it mirrored the individual's coming to the Lord Jesus Christ. Just as that was the beginning of God's work in this man's life, so when you come to Christ it is only the beginning of God's work in your life. And there, in a sense, the real problem begins.

There is an old saying, "It is easy to take a boy out

of the country, but it is hard to get the country out of the boy." That exactly describes God's problem with Abraham. He called him out of the land of Ur of the Chaldees, but it is hard to get Chaldea out of Abraham. It may not be difficult for some to come to Christ. But to get the old man subdued, to get the flesh controlled, and to learn instead to walk in the Spirit—that is what takes grace. It is a process of heartache, interspersed with seasons of joy and blessing. The flesh dies hard and subtly fights back, inventing a thousand and one excuses to get us to leave it alone. But God never leaves us alone. I often rejoice in this in my own Christian life; the faithfulness of God will never let us stop short of the goal he has in mind, which is perfection, the image of Christ.

Now in the closing section of chapter 21 we have a scene of relative quiet and peace. There are three different stories in this section: The story of Hagar and Ishmael out in the wilderness; the story of Abraham and Abimelech making a covenant; and finally, the scene of Abraham and his family living around the well, enjoying the fullness of God. The well is the central theme in each story. It would be easy to dismiss this as an unimportant detail in Abraham's life, except that nothing is unimportant in the Word of God. As Paul says, "All these things . . . were written down for our instruction" (1 Corinthians 10:11). There is nothing included, even though it may seem trivial, that isn't there because it illustrates or helps us to grasp some needed concept of spiritual life. So as you study your Bibles, be sure you learn how to interpret Scripture by Scripture. When you do, the scene becomes clearer.

The spiritual significance of this well is easy to identify, since it occurs frequently in the Bible to picture the Word of God. The water in the well is Christ in his refreshing aspect, the source of refreshment to the thirsty soul. Remember how the Lord said to the woman of Samaria as she came down to the well, "The water that I shall give him will become in him a spring of water welling up to eternal life" (John 4:14b). Wells in Scripture often picture that relationship.

With that as our clue, let us look at these stories and see how the well of Christ appears in various ways. The first one is what we might call the "well of promise."

> *So Abraham rose early in the morning, and took bread and a skin of water, and gave it to Hagar, putting it on her shoulder, along with the child, and sent her away. And she departed, and wandered in the wilderness of Beersheba. When the water in the skin was gone, she cast the child under one of the bushes. Then she went, and sat down over against him a good way off, about the distance of a bow-shot; for she said, "Let me not look upon the death of the child." And as she sat over against him, the child lifted up his voice and wept.*

The boy was more than just a little boy at this point; he was about fourteen years old.

> *And God heard the voice of the lad; and the angel of God called to Hagar from heaven, and said to her, "What troubles you, Hagar? Fear not; for God has heard the voice of the lad where he is. Arise, lift up the lad, and hold him fast with your hand; for I will make him a great nation." Then God opened her eyes, and she saw a well of water; and she went, and filled the skin with water, and gave the lad a drink. And God was with the lad, and he grew up; he lived in the wilderness, and became an expert with the bow. He lived in the wilderness of Paran; and his mother took a wife for him from the land of Egypt (Genesis 21:14-21).*

Much telescopes together in this passage, but we need to understand what this means beyond the mere history of an event. In Galatians, Paul tells us how to interpret Hagar and Ishmael, what they mean to us in the program of God. He says, "Hagar is [a picture of] Mt. Sinai in Arabia" (Galatians 4:25), from which the law was given. She, along with Ishmael, stands for the present Jerusalem, that is, the nation of Israel which refused Christ and yet retained the promises and God's preserving care in their lives. Israel persecuted all those within the nation who turned to Christ in the early days of the church. In Romans, Paul tells us that after the nation had rejected Christ, blindness came upon a part of Israel which would last until all the Gentiles who would believe had come in (Romans 11:25). Here in the Old Testament, two thousand years before our Lord came, this was foretold in the life of Abraham. The New Testament simply confirms what the Old Testament portrays. (This is what ties the Testaments together so we know that both are equally from the hand of God.)

Like Ishmael, the nation of Israel has wandered in the wilderness of the world ever since the day the people said during Passion Week as they gathered before Pilate, "We do not want this man to reign over us" (Luke 19:14b). And "His blood be on us and on our children!" (Matthew 27:25b). So they turned and asked for a robber to be released in the place of Jesus.

Some time afterwards the city of Jerusalem was destroyed, the temple ransacked and demolished, and Israel was driven out into the nations. They wandered like Ishmael in the desert for centuries, without any central place of gathering, without any of the real worship of God they once knew back in Old Testament days. They have been wandering in the wilderness ever since, perishing with thirst.

But a day is coming, as the New Testament tells us, when their eyes will be opened—just as Hagar's eyes were opened here, and she saw the well. The well, remember, is the Word of God, portraying Jesus Christ, the Son of God. Perhaps we are nearing the very hour when Israel, the nation which has been wandering in unbelief ever since that time, will have its eyes opened and behold Christ once again in its own Scriptures. Many have asked why the Jews do not believe in Christ if the Old Testament is so full of him. The answer is that a "hardening has come upon part of Israel." Not all Jews refuse to believe, but many of them, even with the testimony of their own Scriptures, do not believe Jesus is the Messiah. But God says that a day will come at last when their eyes will be opened and they will see in the Word the very one they had once rejected, and Israel will turn to the Lord. They will be refreshed with blessing and they will inhabit the earth; God will be with them, and like Ishmael here, he will make them a great nation again. That is all portrayed in this little scene.

In the next section we have the well appearing in a different aspect, one of great interest to us. This is what we might call the "well of contention."

At that time Abimelech and Phicol the commander of his army said to Abraham, "God is with you in all that you do; now therefore swear to me here by God that you will not deal falsely with me or with my offspring or with my posterity, but as I have dealt loyally with you, you will deal with me and with the land where you have sojourned." And Abraham said, "I will swear." When Abraham complained to Abimelech about a well of water which Abimelech's servants had seized, Abimelech said, "I do not know who has done this thing; you did not tell me, and I have not heard of it until today." So Abraham took sheep and oxen and gave them to Abimelech, and the two men made a covenant. Abraham set seven ewe lambs of the flock apart. And Abimelech said to Abraham, "What. is the meaning of these seven ewe lambs which you have set apart?" He said, "These seven ewe lambs you will take from my hand, that you may be a witness for me that I dug this well." Therefore that place was called Beersheba; because there both of them swore an oath { Beersheba means "the well of the oath."]. So they made a covenant at Beersheba. Then Abimelech and Phicol the commander of his army rose up and returned to the land of the Philistines (Genesis 21:22-32).

What do you make of that? Isn't it a strange thing to be recorded here? We have met Abimelech, the king of the Philistines, before. The name of his commander, the general of his army, was Phicol. Phicol means, "the voice of all." Throughout the Scriptures the Philistine nation pictures the natural man concerned with religious matters, but exercising authority as though he were the voice of all.

In the light of the rise of the ecumenical movement of our own day and its claim to speak for all Protestantism, this exchange between Abraham and Abimelech is very interesting. Abimelech said in effect to Abraham, "I don't understand you evangelicals, yet it is evident that God is with you. You are a mystery to me. You have a remarkable power to stir people up and to upset the apple cart. Because of this I would like you to promise me something. After all, we Philistines are just as religious as you are, but we have different objectives. You are a pilgrim in the land, a sojourner; you don't want to stay here. You keep talking about a city which has foundations that we haven't yet seen. We are not interested in that city, but we have cities of our own right here, and we have great plans and programs to develop them and to make them nice places to live. Now, Abraham, I want you to promise me you won't get involved in our programs and plans and mess everything up. Will you promise me that? You have a lot of power and you are a strange person, but please promise me this."

Abraham said, "I'll be glad to. I have no interest in your programs or your politics—but Abimelech, there is one little thing that bothers me." Abimelech said, "What's that?" And Abraham said, "See this well? It represents to me the Book of God. This is the place of refreshment, where my soul meets God. And you know, your men have been trying to take this away from me."

Abimelech said, "Oh, no, we wouldn't do that. I've never heard a charge like this before. We never meant to take this well away from you. Don't say that."

Then Abraham says, "Now look, Abimelech, I want you to know how much this well means to me. You see those seven little ewe lambs over there? I want you to take those and offer them up as a perpetual reminder that this well means life or death to me. Whenever you think of taking the lives of those seven little lambs, remember that is what this well means to me. It means life to me in this land. I cannot give up this well because this is the source of everything; my refreshment, my strength, and my wisdom. I have need of the well. I found it myself. I dug it. I cannot give it up."

Now let's leave the story here for a minute and see its interpretation in our own lives. I find it significant

that throughout the Christian centuries the disagreement between the world church and real believers in
God has always centered upon the "well of God," the
book of God. The well always pictures the Word of
God, containing and holding in it the waters of refreshment which speak of Christ to the soul. Regardless of different views of the Bible's inspiration, real
believers in Christ have never been able to give up the
book. Here is what God has given us—a well in
which we can find that which ministers to the deep,
deep need of our soul.

This has always been the ground of struggle and
quarreling and disagreement with worldly religious
groups—those who make authoritative pronounce-
ments and declare that this Book is nothing but sage
literature, or mythology, or a collection of old Hebrew stories put together, and that it has no supernatural significance. They deny its prophetic import
and its ability to set forth a supernatural God involv-
ing himself in human life. Throughout the history of
the Christian church, this is where the struggle has
been.

Now to be very practical, this brings us to a problem we face today. I think we can receive some real
help in solving this problem from this story of
Abraham and Abimelech. How much should a Christian get involved in the social programs and improve-
ment policies of worldly religious groups? That is a
problem we are facing today, isn't it? We recognize
there are great injustices in our world. There are terrible, terrible conditions prevailing in our world, not
only in other parts of the globe but here in our own
land. To what extent should we involve ourselves in
programs aimed at correcting these social ills?

Let's take a lesson from dear old Abraham.
Abimelech said to him, "Now Abraham, you don't

think like we do. You have a different objective." I'm amazed at the insight of this man. He at least saw this about Abraham's life. "You are here as a pilgrim and a stranger passing through, a sojourner. Now, Abraham, please promise that you won't get involved."

And Abraham said, "I'll be glad to." More and more I think this is the position Christians must take today. I want to be clear about this because misunderstanding can easily come. It is a case of the good being an enemy of the best. All these social programs are very good things and we cannot deny that a Christian is definitely responsible before God for doing all that he can to alleviate human misery and suffering. If we are not doing that, we are like the Levite and Pharisee in the parable of the good Samaritan (see Luke 10:33). Our Lord taught us to respond to these needs.

Nevertheless, we must not get deeply involved in the programs or the politics. If we do, we have no time left to be what we are supposed to be here on earth. God never called the church to advance human and political liberty. This isn't what the church is here for. It is true that everywhere the church has gone preaching the gospel of Christ, greater liberty has followed. But that is because the church has created an atmosphere in which these liberties can exist. This is the central theme the Word of God would bring out here. Righteous Abraham, living in this land of the Philistines, was a greater source of strength in defense against the enemy of that land simply by being there and being what he was—a man of God in the midst of that scene—than all the plans, programs, armies, and defenses they were concerned about.

This is true today as well. Our Lord tells us we are

to be salt in the earth. We are to be concerned about
changing and transforming men's lives by preaching
the gospel. When the church gives itself to this task
it discovers that it has created an atmosphere in
which political freedom can flourish. Without that
atmosphere, no amount of effort, organizing, committees, programming, and policy-making can ever
succeed in establishing it. When we turn from the
best to the next best, good as that may be, we are
wasting the time God has called us to invest which
will make all the rest possible.

This is confirmed, I think, in the last section. We
read in verses 33-34:

> *Abraham planted a tamarisk tree in Beersheba,*
> *and called there on the name of the* LORD, *the*
> *Everlasting God. And Abraham sojourned many*
> *days in the land of the Philistines.*

This last scene speaks of the "well of communion."
Here is old Abraham planting a tree and living by his
well. Why are we told this? It symbolizes what is taking place in his heart and life. The tree immediately
brings to mind that first Psalm which says of the man
of God, that he shall "be like a tree planted by rivers
of living water, bringing forth its fruit in season."
Here is a fruitful life, concerned about those immediately around, pouring blessing into their lives.

Abraham calls on the name of Yahweh, the everlasting God. I am increasingly convinced that if the
church desires to do anything to help this poor,
blind, bleeding, struggling world, it needs to live
daily in the strength, the power, the purpose, and the
glory of calling upon the everlasting God. This is
what creates joy in our hearts, joy which the world is
so vainly seeking.

I had the privilege to speak on the radio one afternoon in Southern California on 1 Corinthians 10:13:

> No *temptation has overtaken you that is not common to man. God is faithful, and he will not let you be tempted beyond your strength, but with the temptation will also provide the way of escape, that you may be able to endure it.*

My concluding point was that in the midst of the hottest trials, God has provided a way of escape—not from the trials, but from defeat by the trials. The "way" is through rediscovering fellowship with Christ in the trials, just as those three Hebrew children found in the fiery furnace when the king looked in and found a fourth form there, "like a son of the gods" (Daniel 3:25). God didn't take them out of the furnace, but he was in there with them.

When I returned home, I received a letter from a man who had taken a whole sheet of paper and scrawled across the front of it this one sentence: "Dear Mr. Stedman: If it is true that God gives us grace to bear all our trials, then why is it there are so many long-faced Christians?" I thought that was a good letter. My answer was another question. "Dear Sir: If it is true the American soap companies have provided all the soap that we need in this world, why is it that there are so many dirty people?" The answer, of course, is that we are not using the soap that has been provided. The reason for long-faced and dour Christians is that we are not finding the joy of the Lord anymore.

Abraham did find joy, and thus became the center of blessing to the Philistines. In finding and rediscovering those springs of spiritual strength, he did more to advance the cause of social justice and welfare in that land than any Philistine programs and plans could have done.

Our world is looking for reality more today than ever before. The world is desperately searching for men and women of conviction who will stand for what they believe and who will not hesitate to declare it and to say "No" when it means involvement with something they believe is wrong.

The world is searching for men and women who have convictions; and convictions come only from a life involved in living fellowship with a living God. This is what sent that new church in New Testament days out with such triumphant victory over every obstacle. They swept everything before them because they were in daily fellowship with the living God.

We must not leave the best for something less. That would be like a crowd of waiters in a restaurant going back to the kitchen and saying to the cook, "Look, cookie, we are having problems in getting this food out to these people. Why don't you leave the stove and come out here and help us?" If the cook is wise, he will say to them, "Fellows, the worst thing I could do would be to go out to help you. It is true that you have a problem and you have to work it out, but if someone is not here cooking, there will not be anything to distribute."

If there is no fountain of morality in the church, if there are not lives which are discovering the strength and inner peace and power that comes from fellowship with Christ and a living God, there will not be anything to distribute. God calls us to discharge our duties as citizens and to do all we can when we have spare time to help. But by all means let us give ourselves anew to this supreme task of the church of

Christ, which is the declaring of the good news of Jesus Christ, that men may be saved and their lives transformed by coming to know a living God.

16
LIFE'S
HARDEST TRIAL

(Genesis 22:1-19)

Of all the trials in life, there is one that is perhaps harder than all others. It is to this incident in the life of Abraham that we now arrive. One of the most famous stories in the Bible is found in the twenty-second chapter of Genesis—the story of Abraham offering up Isaac. This remarkable Old Testament account foreshadows the work of Christ in the New. It seems to me that no one watching old Abraham binding his dear son to the altar, his heart breaking within him, can miss the parallel with God sending his own Son to Calvary's mountain centuries later.

I want to touch on that aspect as we go through this story, but I wish primarily to dwell on the individual

application to our own hearts. As we have been studying the life of Abraham, we've seen God has written
this man's story in such a way that he is a "pattern man"
of faith, that is, the *Pilgrim's Progress* of the Old Testament. All these incidents recorded in Abraham's life
form clear pictures for us of what occurs in our life of
faith.

In chapters 22 and 23 we come to the story of
Abraham's greatest trial. This is the deepest thrust of
the cross of Christ into his life. Because it was the
work of the cross, there is involved in this account a
Gethsemane, a Calvary, and a resurrection.

> *After these things God tested Abraham, and said
> to him, "Abraham!" And he said, "Here am I."
> He said, "Take your son, your only son Isaac,
> whom you love, and go to the land of Moriah, and
> offer him there as a burnt offering upon one of the
> mountains of which I shall tell you." So Abraham
> rose early in the morning, saddled his ass, and took
> two of his young men with him, and his son Isaac;
> and he cut the wood for the burnt offering, and
> arose and went to the place of which God had told
> him. On the third day Abraham lifted up his eyes
> and saw the place afar off (Genesis 22:1-4).*

It is helpful to realize that about twenty years have
elapsed between chapters 21 and 22. We last saw
Abraham in a tent by the well of Beersheba in the wilderness with his son Isaac. There he worshiped on an
altar he built, calling on the name of the everlasting,
unchangeable God. For twenty years of blessing and
happiness Isaac has been the delight of his parents'
hearts. True to his name, he has brought laughter
into their tent; the whole family life centers around
this dear boy as he grows up to young manhood. Suddenly, like a thunderbolt from the sky, comes this

word from God. Abraham can hardly believe his ears:
God says, "Now take your son Isaac, your only son
whom you love, and go to Mount Moriah and offer
him up on that mountain."

Mount Moriah is the very place where in later years
King David bought the threshing floor of Ornan as a
site of the temple (1 Chronicles 21:18). On that very
place where Abraham offered Isaac, the temple of
Solomon was built (2 Chronicles 3:1). Today there
stands in that place the Dome of the Rock, a Moslem
shrine, built over the great rock that formed the altar
upon which Abraham offered Isaac. It is from this
rock that the Muslims believe Mohammed and his
horse ascended to heaven. It is a very historic spot.

You can imagine what a blow this was to
Abraham. It is specifically called a test. That means
it was meant by God to determine if Abraham's confidence is in his son Isaac, or in God who gave him his
son. This is a test of Abraham's real heart love. Will
Abraham obey the first commandment, "You shall
love the LORD your God with all your heart, and with
all your soul, and with all your mind"? (Matthew
22:37). This is also a test of how far this man has advanced in the life of faith and in the strength of the
Spirit.

The account says nothing about Abraham's emotional reaction to God's request. Perhaps it was quite
unnecessary to say anything. We instinctively know
what this must have meant to Abraham. His first
reaction must have been incredulity. How could God
ask this? And yet the voice is unmistakable; he has
heard this voice many times. Every now and then an
account appears in the newspaper that someone has
heard "the voice of God" telling him to go murder a
certain person. We read of terrible murders carried
out in the mistaken belief that God has ordered

them. But there is nothing like that occurring here.
It is clear from the complete account that God never
had any intention of allowing this to be carried
through, but it was a very severe and bitter test to
determine where Abraham's love was centered.

God is a jealous God, very concerned that he has
what he deserves—that is, first place in every human
heart. You can imagine the questions that must have
arisen in Abraham's mind as he contemplated what
God had asked of him. What about the promises—
all that God had said would take place—what about
those? God has said: "Take your son and offer him as
a burnt offering." "But LORD," Abraham might have
said, "How will the promises be fulfilled that my seed
should fill the land and be as numerous as the stars in
the heavens and the sand on the seashore? Why
should this be asked of me?"

Whenever we get into a strait like this, the question in our hearts is always *Why?* Why should God
do this? Why should it be asked of me?

"I can see, God, why you asked me, your servant
Abraham, to give up Ishmael. You told me to cast
him out of the tent because he was the son of the flesh,
not of promise." We can understand when God tells
us to get rid of some cherished attitude that we know
is wrong. We never ask why about that.

"But, LORD," Abraham may have said, "this is
Isaac; this is the son of promise, this is the one you
yourself gave me. Why do you ask me to put him to
death like this—the very gift of your grace to my
heart?" And then Satan must have suggested doubts
to him, so that he wondered, "How can I find
strength to do this? And what about Sarah? What is
she going to say when I come back from that mountain empty-handed and she asks me what happened?
I'll have to invent some kind of yarn to explain it and

I know she won't believe me. She'll keep probing till she finds out the answer, and how then am I going to face her?" These must have been some of his questions. What a sleepless, troubled night of torture and heartbreak this man went through!

And yet, is it not also a picture for us of that awful struggle in the garden of Gethsemane when our Lord Jesus faced this very same test? God was requiring something of him which God surely could not be asking.

I think to a lesser degree you and I have had experiences like this. Perhaps you have stared in unbelief at some situation in your life and said, "Is this what God wants me to go through? Is this what God is asking of me? Is this God's will?" And your heart cries out, "Why, why should this happen to me?" *This* is life's hardest trial; it is never so difficult when we can see a reason. But when something happens to us in which we fail to see any logic; when, in fact, everything seems to be against it—this is when faith is really put to the test.

Now notice that when morning comes, Abraham's obedience is prompt and complete. Though his heart is torn, yet he obeys God. He has passed the test. I am tremendously impressed at the obedience of this man Abraham. Is not this the secret of his life? We are so inclined to excuse ourselves from hard things and to rationalize our way out of difficult situations, relieving the pressure and avoiding unpleasant situations. We don't like disturbing questions or unsettling challenges. When it comes right down to it, we don't like to take hold of ourselves and say, "I am going to obey God!"

As I have lived, prayed, and studied through the years, I have discovered that God is an utter and complete realist. He is not at all impressed with our emotional, hysterical outbursts. We sometimes get all worked up, and believe our emotions will melt the heart of God and change his mind. But God knows that when he tells us to do something it is necessary—for our benefit, for his benefit, and for everyone concerned. He expects us to obey. I am impressed with Abraham's obedience here; when he hears God tell him to offer his son as a burnt offering on yonder mountain, Abraham obeys.

Now we come to faith's Calvary:

> *Then Abraham said to his young men, "Stay here with the ass; I and the lad will go yonder and worship, and come again to you." And Abraham took the wood of the burnt offering, and laid it on Isaac his son; and he took in his hand the fire and the knife. So they went both of them together. And Isaac said to his father Abraham, "My father!" And he said, "Here am I, my son." He said, "Behold, the fire and the wood; but where is the lamb for a burnt offering?" Abraham said, "God will provide himself the lamb for a burnt offering, my son." So they went both of them together.*

> *When they came to the place of which God had told him, Abraham built an altar there, and laid the wood in order, and bound Isaac his son, and laid him on the altar, upon the wood. Then Abraham put forth his hand, and took the knife to slay his son. But the angel of the LORD called to him from heaven, and said, "Abraham, Abraham!" And he said, "Here am I." He said, "Do not lay your hand on the lad or do anything to him; for now I know that you fear God, seeing you have not withheld your son, your only son, from me." And Abraham lifted up his eyes and looked, and be-*

> *hold, behind him was a ram, caught in a thicket*
> *by his horns; and Abraham went and took the*
> *ram, and offered it up as a burnt offering instead*
> *of his son. So Abraham called the name of that*
> *place "The LORD will provide;" as it is said to this*
> *day, "On the mount of the LORD it shall be pro-*
> *vided" (Genesis 22:5-14).*

Again the record is silent about the emotional reaction of Abraham here, but we have only to put ourselves in his place to sense what he felt, how his heart was torn, how he avoids telling Isaac the fearful truth until the very last possible moment; how he perhaps trembles within when Isaac asks the question, "Where is the lamb?" We know there is no real answer to Isaac's question until we run through intervening centuries and listen in the New Testament to John the Baptist standing before the people of Israel saying, "Behold, the Lamb of God, who takes away the sin of the world" (John 1:29). Just as our Lord Jesus approached his cross with calmness and quiet self-control, so there is a seeming sense of peace about this man Abraham as he draws nearer the actual sacrifice of Isaac.

How can we explain this? Where did this stricken father find the strength to carry through this fearsome task? How did he nerve himself to do it? The answer is found in one brief phrase in verse 5: "Then Abraham said to his young men, 'Stay here with the ass; I and the lad will go yonder and worship, *and come again to you.*'" They would *both* be coming back again. Abraham is not trying to deceive these men, but somewhere in the quiet meditations of that awful night when this word first came to him, there came the consciousness that God could do something to raise this boy from the dead—and Abraham believed in resurrection. That is where he found the peace to follow God's command. In the struggles of that night, he began to reason and to reckon on God.

He must have thought something like this: "God has given me promises and I have lived with God long enough to know that when God gives a promise, he carries it through. God has said that in my son, Isaac, all the nations of the earth shall be blessed. Isaac is necessary to the fulfillment of the promise. It can't be any other; this boy is the one who is going to fulfill the promise. Well, then, if God has asked me now to offer him up as a sacrifice, there is only one explanation. God intends to raise him from the dead."

Abraham had never had, as we have today, the experience or the record of anyone having risen from the dead. He knew nothing of Easter, nor of Lazarus, nor the miracles in the Gospel accounts. Yet so firm is his faith in the character of God that he comes to believe in the resurrection. This is confirmed in Hebrews 11: "By faith Abraham . . . offered up Isaac . . . He considered that God was able to raise men even from the dead; hence, figuratively speaking, he did receive him back" (vs. 19).

As this father is traveling on the way to Mt. Moriah, in his eyes Isaac has been as good as dead for three days. Abraham risked everything he owned and loved upon the character of God; and he found him to be a God of resurrection.

Because of this wonderful triumph in his life, he calls this place, "God will provide." Because of this miracle there sprang up a little saying in Israel, a proverb: "When you get to the mount, it will be provided." Man's disappointments are God's appointments. It is never too late for God. Even if Abraham had been called upon to carry the bloody business

through to its end, nevertheless, his father's heart
was quiet in restful peace because he knew God
would raise his son from the dead. He had promised;
therefore it must be.

Finally, we read of the hope of resurrection morning:

> And the angel of the LORD called to Abraham a
> second time from heaven, and said, "By myself I
> have sworn, says the LORD, because you have done
> this, and have not withheld your son, your only
> son, I will indeed bless you, and I will multiply
> your descendants as the stars of heaven and as the
> sand which is on the seashore. And your descend-
> ants shall possess the gate of their enemies, and by
> your descendants shall all the nations of the earth
> bless themselves, because you have obeyed my voice."
> So Abraham returned to his young men, and they
> arose and went together to Beersheba; and
> Abraham dwelt at Beersheba (Genesis 22:15-
> 19).

When Abraham gave his son back to God, then
God said the promise of fruitfulness would be immediately fulfilled. There would be no more delay.
The rivers of living waters would now begin to flow
from him to bless all the nations of the earth. It was
when Isaac came back from the dead, so to speak, in
resurrection power that God said, "Now the fruitfulness of your life will be manifest." This is resurrection
life.

Even God's gifts to us are of no value until we are
willing, if necessary, to lose them so that God might
reign without a rival. When we have come to that
place to which the Spirit of God wants to bring us,
that perfect relationship with the Father in which our
Lord lived his entire life . . . when God means more

to us than anything . . . when we love the Lord our God with all our strength and soul and mind and spirit and heart, and we are even willing to give up the very gift that God has given—then in resurrection power that gift will be a blessing to everyone it touches.

God has given gifts to us all. Maybe God has given you a special talent and you are asked to take a job where perhaps you can't use that talent. You wonder about it, and perhaps rebel over it. But remember Abraham, and give it back to God. Face the possibility of not using that talent, and the God of resurrection will take that talent and return it to you and make it a blessing to many hearts. Anything else will be a curse.

Perhaps you have a loved one and a situation arises in which you have to part from him or break that relationship. This is a struggle, but Abraham's faith said that if God asks you to do it, then there is blessing beyond if you obey. Maybe you are living in a situation of comfort and happiness but you are needed in another place which is not as pleasant, and you say, "Lord, why— why do I have to give up my home and my relationships which I enjoy?" You resist, you question, as Abraham did. Remember, however, that if God calls, you must obey. Beyond the apparent heartbreak and death lies resurrection. In the resurrection of that experience, God will give you back that gift and make it a blessing.

Is not this the record of every man and woman whose life has ever counted for God, who have been willing to give up the very areas they thought were God's choice blessing for them when God called? In so doing, God made them a blessing. It can be in minor or major areas. This is the principle of the cross throughout all our lives. This is what makes resurrection life possible. This is why the Lord Jesus says, "He who loves father or mother . . . son or daughter more than me is not worthy of me. He who finds his life will lose it, and he who loses his life for my sake will find it" (Matthew 10:39).

Our God is the God of resurrection. When it looks as though we are throwing away every chance of blessing, God transforms in a moment the very thing we give up into the most richly rewarding and meaningful experience we have ever had. I dare you to act upon this. I don't know what it might be for you, but I know this is true and that God has written this account so we may know this is his way in the affairs of men. When we dare to stand upon what God has said, we discover as Paul did that the yearning of our hearts is "that I may know him and the power of his resurrection, and may share his sufferings, becoming like him in his death" (Philippians 3:10).

17
'TILL DEATH
DO US PART

(Genesis 23)

What a bitter day it is when a man buries his wife!
It is perhaps the lowest point ever reached by the
human spirit, and the sunset for him of all earth's
hopes and expectations. In Genesis 23 we stand beside Abraham as he weeps at the grave of Sarah. He is
walking through the valley where death has cast its
shadow, but we shall see as we read this chapter that
there is a light which always shines through the dark
shadows in the life of a man of faith. As we sometimes
sing in the old hymn, "There is a light in the valley of
death now for me, since Jesus came into my heart."

The first two verses of chapter 23 bring us into the
shadow of heartache and death.

*Sarah lived a hundred and twenty-seven years;
these were the years of the life of Sarah. And Sarah
died at Kiriath-arba {that is, Hebron} in the
land of Canaan; and Abraham went in to mourn
for Sarah and to weep for her (Genesis 23:1,2).*

Probably about seventeen years have passed between chapter 22 and chapter 23. These accounts of
Abraham's trials follow consecutively in the sacred
record, but they are separated by many years of blessing, tranquility and peace. Sarah was one hundred
and twenty-seven years old when she died; and Isaac,
her son, is now forty-seven. By this time the little
family of Abraham, Sarah and Isaac had moved back
from Beersheba to Hebron, under the oak of Mamre,
where they had first lived when they came into the
land of Canaan—rather like going back to their hon-
eymoon cottage—and here Sarah died. In one respect
this was a wonderful place to die. As the place names
indicate, it is in the place of "fatness" of soul and richness of fellowship with the Lord that Sarah, this
woman of beauty and faith, dies.

As was customary in those days, the body of Sarah
was placed in a tent all by itself and into that tent
goes Abraham alone to weep and mourn. It is remarkable that this is the only time we are ever told
that Abraham wept. This old man has gone through
many, many bitter disappointments and times of
heartbreak. He was disappointed when Lot left him.
He was heartbroken when Ishmael was sent out. His
heart was torn with anguish when he had to offer
Isaac upon the mountain. But the only time the record reveals that he wept was when Sarah died. I
think this reveals the depth of his grief and love for
this woman.

It may be revealing for us to spend a few moments

here with Abraham as he bows over the body of Sarah. As you perhaps already know, if you have wept with Abraham, the well of grief is fed by the springs of memory. All the dear, sweet days come crowding in upon us, just as they must have to Abraham. I think he saw in his mind's eye that beautiful girl who captured his heart long, long ago. I think it was in the spring, for even back in those days in the spring a young man's fancy turned to what the young women had been thinking about all winter! "Boy meets girl" was the same wonderful story in the days of Abraham some four thousand years ago as it is today. As the old man wept over the body of Sarah, he must have remembered all those wonderful times.

Memories passed through his mind like pearls on a string. He remembered the sunlight glittering in her hair when he first saw her, the radiance of her face on her wedding day, the softness of her touch, and the grace of her caress. Each remembrance brought heartache in the darkness of his grief. He recalled the high adventure of their life together, and especially that supreme, compelling call from God that sent them out as a couple together into an unknown land. He remembered how Sarah went along with him, sharing hardships, accepting the unsettled life without a murmur or complaint.

How his heart must have rocked with anguish as he remembered anew his perfidy in Egypt when he exposed her to danger and dishonor with his lie before Pharaoh, and again years later before Abimelech! All the bittersweet memories came in upon him as he recalled their long, weary years without a child and how they wept together. He remembered how Sarah cried bitter tears over that barren womb and how in her desperation to give him a son, she offered her handmaid, even at the cost of her pride, and Ishmael was born. All of this must have filled Abraham's heart as he wept here before Sarah.

He remembered, too, how at long last, glory shone in her face when her own son, Isaac, lay in her arms. His memory ran back through the years and retraced the love that drew them together, through the bad times and through the good, till they were one in body, mind, and heart.

Now death has torn her from his arms . . . though it could never tear her from his heart. It is an hour of darkness and grief in the shadow of death. But this is not the whole story. As we read this account, we read something further of the life of faith.

> And Abraham rose up from before his dead, and said to the Hittites, "I am a stranger and a sojourner among you; give me property among you for a burying place, that I may bury my dead out of my sight." The Hittites answered Abraham, "Hear us, my lord; you are a mighty prince among us. Bury your dead in the choicest of our sepulchres; none of us will withhold from you his sepulchre, or hinder you from burying your dead" (Genesis 23:3-6).

I love this phrase, "Abraham rose up from before his dead." That signified a squaring of the shoulder, a lifting of the eye, a firming of the step, a facing of life again, and it is followed by a wonderful confession of faith: "I am a stranger and a sojourner among you." That is the word of a man who looks beyond all that earth has to offer and once more sees the city which has foundations whose builder and maker is God.

Although Abraham has been weeping in the valley of the shadow of death, he somehow senses there can be no shadow without a light somewhere. Have you learned that? When shadows come into your life, it is a sign that there must be light somewhere. Of course, if we turn our back on the light, then we ourselves are the ones who cause the shadow. I think thousands of people today live in constant shadow because their back is turned toward the light and they cast a pall upon themselves. But if we face the light—as Abraham did all through his life, looking at that light streaming from the city whose builder and maker is God— then the only shadow comes temporarily when some object obscures the light for a moment.

After all, that is what death is; it is simply a temporary obscuring of the light. But the man of faith lifts his eyes and looks beyond the shadow and sees the light still shining, and he says to those people, "I am a stranger and a sojourner among you. Nothing satisfies me down here. I can never settle down among you." The whole land had been given to him by the promise of God, but the dead body of his wife before him reminds him that it is not yet God's time. His faith is not weakened by the death which occurred here, but rather, it is strengthened by it.

If Abraham had not remembered that he was a pilgrim and a stranger, his heart would have been crushed to despair by the death of his beloved life's companion. So many, many people seem to come to the end of existence when some loved one passes on, someone with whom their hearts are closely bound. But Abraham lifts his eyes beyond this to the light from the city beyond. He remembers that nothing in this life was ever intended to fully meet the needs of the heart of the pilgrim-stranger passing through. He confesses that fact here again in his hour of grief.

I recall hearing Dr. Barnhouse relate an interesting incident that illustrates this very point. He told of a girl whose husband had been killed in action during the war. When the telegram came, this Christian girl read it through and then said to her mother, "Mother, I am going up to my room and please don't disturb me." Her mother called the father at work and told him what had happened. He came hurrying home and immediately went up to the room. He opened the door quietly. The room was carpeted and the girl didn't hear him come in, and he saw her kneeling beside her bed. The telegram was spread open on the bed before her. She was bowed over it. And as he stood there, he heard her say, "Oh, my heavenly Father, Oh, my Father, my heavenly Father." Without a word the man turned around and went back down the stairs and said to his wife, "She is in better hands than mine."

This is what faith does in the hour of grief. The very strength of Abraham's faith in the midst of anguish is that he is a stranger and a sojourner, a pilgrim passing through to that city which can alone satisfy the human heart.

Now in the following verses we see something of the independence of the man of faith:

> Abraham rose and bowed to the Hittites, the people of the land. And he said to them, "If you are willing that I should bury my dead out of my sight, hear me, and entreat for me Ephron the son of Zohar, that he may give me the cave of Machpelah, which he owns; it is at the end of his field. For the full price let him give it to me in your presence as a possession for a burying place." Now Ephron was sitting among the Hittites; and Ephron the Hittite answered Abraham in the hearing of the Hittites, of all who went in at the gate of his city, "No, my lord, hear me; I give you the field, and I give you

the cave that is in it; in the presence of the sons of my people I give it to you; bury your dead." Then Abraham bowed down before the people of the land. And he said to Ephron in the hearing of the people of the land, "But if you will, hear me; I will give the price of the field; accept it from me, that I may bury my dead there." Ephron answered Abraham, "My lord, listen to me; a piece of land worth four hundred shekels of silver, what is that between you and me? Bury your dead." Abraham agreed with Ephron; and Abraham weighed out for Ephron the silver which he had named in the hearing of the Hittites, four hundred shekels of silver, according to the weights current among the merchants.

So the field of Ephron in Machpelah, which was to the east of Mamre, the field with the cave which was in it and all the trees that were in the field, throughout its whole area, was made over to Abraham as a possession in the presence of the Hittites, before all who went in at the gate of his city. After this, Abraham buried Sarah his wife in the cave of the field of Machpelah east of Mamre {that is, Hebron} in the land of Canaan. The field and the cave that is in it were made over to Abraham as a possession for a burying place by the Hittites (Genesis 23:7-20).

Why does Scripture go into all this detail? For one thing, this is the one place among many doubtful sites in the land of Palestine that has been authenticated today. We can still visit the cave of Machpelah in Israel. There Abraham and Sarah lie buried together. There Jacob and Leah lie together. There has been a great mosque erected above it, but it is very certain that this is the cave in which Abraham lies buried and where he buried Sarah.

The rigamarole that Abraham and Ephron go through in this account is very oriental; they carry on like this today in eastern market places. Abraham's pagan friends do have, however, a genuine sense of respect and honor for the man of faith. "Thou art a prince among us," they say. "Although we recognize that you are different and perhaps this caused many questions at first, yet we know that you are a man of great honor." They pay respectful deference to him, and are quite willing that he have the land.

I think this is remarkable. Though the difference that being a Christian makes may create a feeling of estrangement and even dislike for awhile, it always results at last in the highest respect and honor. Young people, under so much pressure to conform, especially need to hear this. The world is constantly trying to squeeze us into its own mold, and we don't like to be different. Yet the one thing that Christ demands of us is that in the essentials of our lives and attitudes we be different. There are many areas in which we don't need to be different, and may even be offensive by being unnecessarily different. But there are other areas where we must not conform.

When Abraham first came into the land he was a pilgrim and a stranger, and they must have looked upon him as a wandering nomad. It may have taken him a long time to win their respect. But here at the end all these pagan friends gather around and say to him, "Thou art a prince, a mighty prince among us. You can have anything you want. We respect your integrity, your heart, even though you are still a stranger and a sojourner."

But I think the supreme lesson here is to show us the thorough independence of the man of faith. Abraham will not consent to own one foot of ground without paying for it. He courteously insists on taking nothing from the world, though he is ready to take everything from God. He shows a great independence here; he will not allow the world to make him rich in any degree. God had promised him this land and no stratagem of the enemy, no temporary expedient, will satisfy him. It must come from God, and until it does, he insists on paying for this segment of it even though they offer it to him. At the end of his career, although he owned the land by promise, the only part he actually possessed was the field and a cave where he buried his wife. This is a picture of the man of faith.

In the book of Hebrews we are told that none of these men and women of faith in the Old Testament ever really gained the promise for which they were looking. They are still moving toward it, because without us they will not be made perfect. We are called upon to hold this same attitude. Remember, nothing on earth satisfies the pilgrims and strangers passing through this land.

There is a great dearth of rugged individualism in our world today. We are missing it in our American scene. What is the secret of it? We learn from the life of Abraham that the secret is fixing our eye upon another place and not being satisfied with anything that earth offers. Then we can be quite indifferent to the appeals, the claims and the pressures which come from every side. If we are really wrapped up in this scene down here, we are sitting ducks for all the pressures that come, in whatever form. If our eyes are fixed upon that over there—off yonder, where the man of faith looks, the city that God alone makes—then we can be very independent here. This is what we see in Abraham.

As a boy, my heart was mightily stirred when I read the accounts of the Scottish Covenantors in their resistance against the tyranny and totalitarianism of the Roman Catholic church. Their very lives were in danger as they were hounded and hunted throughout the glens and hills of Scotland. Many of them were put to death as martyrs for their faith. It was back in those days that dear old Samuel Rutherford lived, one of those who were subjected to the wrath of the king because of their protestant faith.

The letters of Samuel Rutherford are a wonderful treasury of a devotional life enthralled and captured by Christ. He was a little, but sturdy, man. I remember reading that when he lay dying in prison in St. Andrews, Scotland, the king sent a messenger to summon him to appear in a London court to answer to charges of high heresy. When the messenger came in before the old man as he lay there on his death bed and announced that the king ordered him to appear in court, he said to him in his Scottish fashion, "Gang and tell yere master, I have a summons from a higher court and ere this message reaches him, I'll be where few kings or great folk ever come." It was a stirring rebuke to a man of earth who thought he could summon a man of faith.

This is the kind of individualism that comes from lifting your eyes from the paltry, temporary, transitory, everyday happenings, and setting them on those eternal issues that alone satisfy the heart. This is beautifully demonstrated in this scene from the life of Abraham. Abraham owned a burial cave in the end. That was all. It is a reminder that all we can ever really own down here is a burial ground in which we may lay to rest the hopes and expectations of this life. All we hope for and all the fine things we hope to have someday, all the experiences we would like to live over again, all these expectations, are buried in the grave. If this is all we have, what an empty, pitiful life this has been.

What a wonderful inspiration it is to look at these men of faith in the Old Testament and read again that stirring account in Hebrews 11 of men and women who "went about in skins of sheep and goats, destitute, afflicted, ill-treated—of whom the world was not worthy—wandering over deserts and mountains, and in dens and caves of the earth" (vs. 37b-38). They had none of the comforts that the world counts of great value, but God has recorded of them that they have a great and wonderful future ahead. For them, like Abraham, even the crushing sorrows of earth, the separation from loved ones, cannot dim the light of that hope which streams from the city to come.

We are made to be creatures of eternity. In the book of Ecclesiastes it says that God "put eternity into man's mind" (Ecclesiastes 3:11). We are not made to be creatures of time. We are not made to be satisfied with this brief period of life and then to pass into the endless, silent realms of death. God has set eternity in our hearts. But the great tragedy is that we can so easily lose sight of the goal. We begin to be wrapped up in the problems of time, and we lose the broad view of eternity.

Yet the power available to us enables us to lift a face radiant with life in the midst of the deepest sorrow, to be strong when others are weak, to refuse to give way to panic and fear when the world is trembling and afraid. It all comes from the fact that, like Abraham, we too are pilgrims and strangers. As Paul says, "Set your minds on things that are above, not on things that are on earth" (Colossians 3:2). It is this attitude, this state of mind, that gives strength and grace and peace to the grieving heart.

As we have looked at this scene of Abraham, bowed in grief for the moment over the dead and lifeless body of his dear life companion, our own hearts enter with sympathy into that scene. We know life can often strike with terrible blows; we feel the thrust of it, the hurt of it, the loneliness of it. We know that we can be shaken sometimes by the things which take place. But, thank God, although there are things about us that can be shaken, there are other things that cannot be. When our faith rests upon the finished work of our Lord Jesus, and our hearts have been captured by one who has said that we can never be fully satisfied with what is here below—but our eyes are caught by the light that streams from the city beyond and we press on toward that— then we may be fitted and made ready for that place, mastering lessons for use over there.

18
HERE COMES
THE BRIDE

(Genesis 24)

We are almost at the close of our study in the life of Abraham as we look at chapter 24 of Genesis. Here is the delightful story of Abraham sending his servant to find a wife for his son. The remarkable love story of Rebekah and Isaac is one of those tales which we have all known since childhood as one of the loveliest in the Old Testament. This is more than the old-but-ever-new story of boy meets girl. It has more than that kind of fascination, and certainly it has more than good suggestions on how to get a wife by proxy. It is a story, as we have seen in the incidents from Abraham's life, that has meaning for us as well, although it becomes evident toward the end of

Abraham's life that these incidents break over the boundaries of individual application. They become a picture of the work of God himself.

For example: In the story of the sacrifice of Isaac, it is easy to see how the Spirit of God, two thousand years before our Lord was born, designed the incident to illustrate the Father's heart toward the cross of Calvary. As Abraham and Isaac trudged up the mountainside together, you can see father and son mounting the hill of Calvary and feel the anguish in that father's heart as he gives his own beloved son as a living sacrifice there. These stories become luminous illustrations of New Testament events and truths.

This is true of this story of Rebekah and Isaac. It is a picture of Pentecost. Here is Abraham standing for God the Father, sending his unnamed servant into the far country to take a bride for his son—to invite her to come, to call, to woo, and to win her—to bring her back at last to the father's house where the son waits to claim his bride for himself. How beautifully that portrays God, at the day of Pentecost, sending his Spirit into the world! It is the Spirit's work to call out a people for God's name, to win a bride for Christ; he has been at this task for almost two thousand years, and the Son is waiting to receive that bride. We read in the Book of Revelation about the wedding supper of the Lamb and of the Lord coming to claim his bride for himself (see Revelation 19:7-9).

Still, as good as this general application is, we must not neglect to apply these stories individually. These Old Testament stories are somewhat like dreams. Psychologists tell us that no matter what we dream about, we are always represented. If we dream of an old mule eating hay, that's us. Whatever else our dream may be, somehow we are involved. In some way, this is true of these Old Testament stories.

Paul says, "Now these things happened to them as a warning, but they were written down for our instruction, upon whom the end of the ages has come" (1 Corinthians 10:11). They are not written just for historic reference. They are written to teach us something, and we don't want to miss it. Read your Old Testament with this in view and seek to find what the Spirit of God has for you.

If you are a Christian, where are you in this story of Abraham sending his servant to get a bride for his son Isaac? "Obviously we are the bride," you may say, "we are the ones who are called by the Spirit of God." This is true. Every Christian remembers how he sensed at one time the calling of the Spirit of God. We remember how he wooed and won us by the loveliness and beauties which are in Jesus Christ, and by a consciousness of our utter need for him. We were called to love someone we had never seen, and we felt an answering response in our hearts as Christ was painted in vivid colors by the Spirit in our minds. We felt the urge to leave friends and family behind (in the sense of shifting their central place in our affections), and to go after this one who called us. Now we are journeying to meet him at last in that country in the Father's house. But this does not exhaust the full meaning of this story nor does it really disclose the major emphasis.

If you read this chapter carefully, you will find that the central character is not the bride, Rebekah. Little of her reaction is recorded here; her part is secondary. The spotlight really follows Abraham's servant. He is the central character. This illustrates, we have seen, the Holy Spirit's work. But remember, the Spirit of God chooses to do his work largely through men and women, through believers, through the church, through those of us who are his. This is

especially true in the work of calling out a people for
God's name. God has given us the responsibility and
the privilege of being his instruments to call his bride
out of the world. So this story becomes a beautiful
picture of the whole process of personal evangelism.

The process of bringing others to Christ begins
with the command of God the Father:

> *Now Abraham was old, well advanced in years;
> and the* LORD *had blessed Abraham in all things.
> And Abraham said to his servant, the oldest of his
> house, who had charge of all that he had, "Put
> your hand under my thigh, and I will make you
> swear by the* LORD, *the God of heaven and of the
> earth, that you will not take a wife for my son from
> the daughters of the Canaanites, among whom I
> dwell, but will go to my country and to my
> kindred, and take a wife for my son Isaac." The
> servant said to him, "Perhaps the woman may not
> be willing to follow me to this land* [this man
> knew women]; *must I then take your son back to
> the land from which you came?" Abraham said to
> him, "See to it that you do not take my son back
> there. The* LORD, *the God of heaven, who took me
> from my father's house and from the land of my
> birth, and who spoke to me and swore to me, 'To
> your descendants I will give this land,' he will
> send his angel before you, and you shall take a wife
> for my son from there. But if the woman is not
> willing to follow you, then you will be free from
> this oath of mine; only you must not take my son
> back there." So the servant put his hand under the
> thigh of Abraham his master, and swore to him
> concerning this matter (Genesis 24:1-9).*

The initiative here begins with Abraham. He sends his servant to do this work and binds him to the task with an oath. Putting the hand under the thigh is simply an oriental custom recognizing that the loins were the source of life. For the servant, it represented being bound in the very deepest part of his life. This was a solemn oath. As we apply this to our own situation and see God the Father standing in the place of Abraham here, he is asking every servant to give himself to this task. The servant is unnamed here, I believe, so that you and I can put our names here. We are called by the Father, commanded to go and take a wife for his son.

This is not an option with a believer in Jesus Christ. God has said, not only in the typical fashion we see here, but in many direct and solemn statements in the Word of God that every believer is obligated to reach others for Jesus Christ. God has said, "Take a wife for my son." To this end the Spirit of God has come into our hearts to dwell. His whole purpose of coming into your life and mine is that he might be what he is and do what he came to do. Our Lord Jesus is the one dwelling within and we are told what he came to do. He said, "For the son of man came to seek and to save the lost" (Luke 19:10). If this is what he came to do, we will find him doing it in our lives if we give him the opportunity.

Please notice that the responsibility here is emphasized by the restriction given to the servant. Abraham said to him, "You must not take my son back there. I know how you feel. I know it would be so much easier if you could just take this handsome lad with you. It would be so much easier to convince this girl she ought to come live with him if she could just see him. But don't take Isaac back there!" Why was this odd restriction put upon him? It does seem strange; although it would make the process of courtship so much simpler, he definitely restricts Isaac from going.

This is no ordinary incident; this is divinely planned, and is intended to teach a lasting truth. It illustrates that God's son is now in his glory and the work of evangelism must go forward in his absence. God does not send Jesus visibly back to earth in order to win the church. How much easier it would seem to persuade men and women to believe in him if we could just say, "Well, he is now in San Francisco and we'd love to take you up there so you could just hear him speak and see the marks of the nails in his hands. Then you could believe." We tend to think it would go better that way.

But the Lord said, "No." He sent the Spirit of God to do the work, and in some remarkable way we will never fully understand, the Spirit of God can make Jesus Christ more real to a human heart than if he stood before him in human form and flesh.

Even in the New Testament we discover that when the disciples personally accompanied Jesus, they were constantly confused and frustrated. They could not understand what he said; they were troubled and disturbed time after time. But when the day of Pentecost came and the Spirit of God flooded their souls, a light came into their eyes that blasted away their spiritual blindness. The Scriptures began to open up for them. They became conscious of the reality of Christ and experienced a joy within that they had never known before. It is the work of the Spirit to make Christ real to us. That is why God has laid upon every one of us this obligation to spread his word to others.

There is an imaginary account telling of the time when the Lord ascended into glory. He was met by the angels as he came into the throne room of God, and one of them said to him, "Lord, what are your plans now to propagate the work that you have begun down there? What have you devised to carry on this work in your absence?" The Lord said, "I've called twelve men to follow me and I have taught them and lived with them for three and one-half years. I have left them behind to carry on the work." But the angel said to him, "Lord, what if they fail? What if they don't do the job?" The Lord shook his head and said, "Well, I have no other plan."

While the point of the story is true, I hasten to correct the possible false impression that God has left us to do the job wholly depending upon ourselves. He has not done that. Still, it is true that God has no other plan. He will not send his Son back until the appointed time. Nor will he call the church in any other way. He has put the Spirit of God in our hearts that we might be used in this wonderful work of winning a bride for his son. This is our responsibility, and the command of the Father's heart.

The major emphasis of this passage is centered on what we might call the cooperation of the Spirit. This, I think, is the missing note in much personal evangelism. So many men and women have heard the command of God, "Go into all the world and preach the gospel to the whole creation." They have recognized the command, but then they act as though it all depends upon them. The result is that many show a zeal without knowledge. This is where the buttonholing, grimfaced, fever-eyed fanatic comes from, on the one hand, and on the other, the timid, blushing, flustered Christian who hardly ever dares to utter a word. We fail to recognize that not only has God commanded us to do this, but he has also provided the power by which to do it.

This is what appears in the steps which follow. There are five stages pictured here illustrating what happens when you or I go out to reach someone for Christ. First of all, there is expectation.

Then the servant took ten of his master's camels and departed, taking all sorts of choice gifts from his master; and he arose, and went to Mesopotamia, to the city of Nahor. And he made the camels kneel down outside the city by the well of water at the time of evening, the time when women go out to draw water. And he said, "O LORD, God of my master Abraham, grant me success today, I pray thee, and show steadfast love to my master Abraham. Behold, I am standing by the spring of water, and the daughters of the men of the city are coming out to draw water. Let the maiden to whom I shall say, 'Pray let down your jar that I may drink,' and who shall say, 'Drink, and I will water your camels'—let her be the one whom thou hast appointed for thy servant Isaac. By this I shall know that thou hast shown steadfast love to my master" (Genesis 24:10-14).

Now here is a man expecting God to work. He does not go into this land and say to himself, "Well now, the whole job is up to me. I've got to find this girl, and how in the world am I going to find the right one? And after that, I must persuade her to come. How am I going to do that?"

Why is it so simple for this man? Because he knows he is not left alone to do this task. An invisible partner is at work, preparing the way for him. I wish we could learn this lesson about our own witness. God has not left it to us to do alone. The work of reaching men and women for Christ is not a matter of human persuasion, but is a divine call. God is at work to move, shape, and develop the lives and hearts of all. Our job is simply to recognize this and look for indications of his working.

Do you notice how Abraham's servant does it? First he prays, revealing his expectation that God is at work. In his simple prayer he asks God to make the way clear, to indicate the one to whom God would have him speak. As he prays about his problem, he expects God to answer.

This is a wonderful concept to remember when witnessing. When I get aboard a plane or train to go someplace where I may be in contact with someone who doesn't know the Lord, I ask God to indicate who is the one he wants me to talk with. Maybe there is no one; maybe the Lord wants me to spend my time reading or studying. But very likely he does have someone. I don't know who God is working with, but I know that he will direct me through ways I can hardly guess.

When I get on the plane, I find the best seat first. That is the obvious thing to do. Then I trust that the man who sits down beside me may be that man, or the one in front of me, or the one behind me. But I don't know. It may be the fellow who is to get on at an airport down the line, or the one that I will meet in the aisle, or the flight attendant. I don't know. So how do I find out?

Let's look at the next step. The first step was expectation; the next one is confirmation:

> *Before he had done speaking, behold, Rebekah, who was born to Bethuel the son of Milcah, the wife of Nahor, Abraham's brother, came out with her water jar upon her shoulder. The maiden was very fair to look upon, a virgin, whom no man had known. She went down to the spring, and filled her*

*jar, and came up. Then the servant ran to meet
her, and said, "Pray give me a little water to
drink from your jar." She said, "Drink, my
lord"; and she quickly let down her jar upon her
hand, and gave him a drink. When she had
finished giving him a drink, she said, "I will
draw for your camels also, until they have done
drinking." So she quickly emptied her jar into the
trough and ran again to the well to draw, and she
drew for all his camels. The man gazed at her in
silence to learn whether the LORD had prospered
his journey or not (Genesis 24:15-21).*

Here is the confirmation. The man gazed at her in
silence, we read. If we stopped there we might think
it was because he was so amazed at a teenage girl so
willing to work. I don't know how authentic it is,
but I am told that a camel can drink twenty- one gal-
lons of water at a sitting, and she drew water for all
his camels. No wonder he gazed at her in silence.

Specifically, though, we are told that it was to
learn whether the Lord had prospered his journey or
not. "Is this the one, LORD?" As he watched her, he
knew this was the one, because she did just the thing
he had asked of the Lord as a sign.

I don't think it is wise to ask for particular signs in
every case. Sometimes we invent these signs in our
own mind and use them as an excuse for not witnessing. If we expect God to show us someone to talk
with, he will indicate to us whom he has prepared.

Some years ago I was on my way to Japan, waiting
in the airport at Honolulu for a plane to Tokyo. It
was early in the morning and the airport was almost
deserted. I bought a newspaper to read as I waited for
my flight. In it I read an account of a young Filipino
eye doctor who was in Honolulu on his way home to

Manila. He was a surgeon who had perfected an operation no one else had done, and he had been demonstrating it to some New York doctors. I read through the account along with other things and thought nothing more of it. When the time came, I boarded my plane and sat down in the most comfortable seat to wait for take-off.

Soon a man came along and sat down beside me. I turned to say hello, and saw he was a young Filipino. I still didn't make any connection, but asked his name, and he told me he was a doctor. So I said, "What kind of a doctor are you?" He said, "I'm an eye surgeon." Then I remembered the newspaper account I had just read about this young Filipino eye surgeon, and we had a brief discussion which led quickly to the subject of the Word of God. When I left him, I gave him a New Testament. When I met him later in Manila, he told me he'd been reading it every day since and had given his heart to the Lord.

Here is confirmation, some little thing by which God says, "Here is the one with whom I've been working and here you are beside him." The Lord brought the two together. You can expect wonderful things to happen if you begin to watch for God to work through you like this, alert for indications of the Spirit at work.

After the confirmation comes the third stage, the preparation:

> *When the camels had done drinking, the man took a gold ring weighing a half shekel, and two bracelets for her arms weighing ten gold shekels, and said, "Tell me whose daughter you are. Is there room in your father's house for us to lodge in?" She said to him, "I am the daughter of Bethuel the son of Milcah, whom she bore to*

> *Nahor." She added, "We have both straw and*
> *provender enough, and room to lodge in." The man*
> *bowed his head and worshiped the* LORD, *and*
> *said, "Blessed be the* LORD, *the God of my master*
> *Abraham, who has not forsaken his steadfast love*
> *and his faithfulness toward my master. As for me,*
> *the* LORD *has led me in the way to the house of my*
> *master's kinsmen" (Genesis 24:22-27).*

Abraham's servant knows this is the right girl. He has had the sign confirmed. But he doesn't immediately open the Scriptures to Romans 3:23 and begin to blast her with her status as a sinner. He doesn't brashly chasten her with the Lord's wrath and scare her away, as we sometimes do. Nor does he immediately start talking about Isaac. Instead, he wisely arranges for private conversation, allowing sufficient time to make a proper contact. He bathes the whole matter again in prayer and thanksgiving and waits for a suitable time to talk.

Surely this is a very important step. Sometimes in our zeal we jump down people's throats and frighten them, causing them to back away from us. We must remember to take time to lay ample groundwork, and to prepare for a proper presentation. Perhaps an invitation to dinner is better than just leaning over the back fence and trying to give the gospel in five minutes.

The fourth step is the presentation itself. In the next section we shall find the whole story spelled out plainly and frankly.

> *So he said, "I am Abraham's servant. The* LORD
> *has greatly blessed my master, and he has become*
> *great; he has given him flocks and herds, silver and*
> *gold, menservants and maidservants, camels and*
> *asses. And Sarah my master's wife bore a son to my*

*master when she was old; and to him he has given
all that he has. My master made me swear, saying, 'You shall not take a wife for my son from the
daughters of the Canaanites, in whose land I
dwell; but you shall go to my father's house and to
my kindred, and take a wife for my son.' I said to
my master, 'Perhaps the woman will not follow
me.' But he said to me, 'The* LORD, *before whom I
walk, will send his angel with you and prosper
your way; and you shall take a wife for my son
from my kindred and from my father's house; then
you will be free from my oath, when you come to my
kindred; and if they will not give her to you, you
will be free from my oath.'*

"I *came today to the spring, and said, 'O* LORD,
*the God of my master Abraham, if now thou wilt
prosper the way which I go, behold, I am standing
by the spring of water; let the young woman who
comes out to draw, to whom I shall say, "Pray give
me a little water from your jar to drink," and who
will say to me, "Drink, and I will draw for your
camels also," let her be the woman whom the* LORD
has appointed for my master's son.'

"*Before I had done speaking in my heart, behold,
Rebekah came out with her water jar on her shoulder; and she went down to the spring, and drew. I
said to her, 'Pray let me drink.' So I drank, and
she gave the camels drink also. Then I asked her,
'Whose daughter are you?' She said, 'The daughter of Bethuel, Nahor's son, whom Milcah bore to
him.' So I put the ring on her nose, and the
bracelets on her arms. Then I bowed my head and
worshiped the* LORD, *and blessed the* LORD, *the
God of my master Abraham, who had led me by*

the right way to take the daughter of my master's kinsman for his son. Now then, if you will deal loyally and truly with my master, tell me; and if not, tell me; that I may turn to the right hand or to the left."

Then Laban and Bethuel answered, "The thing comes from the LORD; we cannot speak to you bad or good. Behold, Rebekah is before you, take her and go, and let her be the wife of your master's son, as the LORD has spoken."

When Abraham's servant heard their words, he bowed himself to the earth before the LORD. And the servant brought forth jewelry of silver and of gold, and raiment, and gave them to Rebekah; he also gave to her brother and to her mother costly ornaments (Genesis 24:34-53).

The servant leaves nothing out, but is forthright and candid. He begins with the glories of Abraham, telling about all his wealth, flocks, herds, silver and gold, servants, camels, and asses. Why? Because this is the inheritance of the son. Then he recounts how God led him along the way; that is, he gives his own personal testimony about it. He ends by presenting to her the gifts Isaac had sent along, the sample of the riches he was offering to her.

What an illustration of how we should talk to those who are interested and whom the Lord is seeking to reach—by focusing it all on Christ! Our work is not to change people's habits. We are not out to get people to stop drinking, smoking, dancing, going to movies, etc. That isn't our concern. Our task is to win them to Christ, not to make church members out of them. This servant did not go into the far country and try to start a "Fans for Isaac Club."

His job was to win her heart and bring her out of the far country to the son; and that is our work, also.

The fifth and last stage is the actual invitation:

> *And he and the men who were with him ate and drank, and they spent the night there. When they arose in the morning, he said, "Send me back to my master." Her brother and her mother said, "Let the maiden remain with us a while, at least ten days; after that she may go."* [There was a reluctance to let her go.] *But he said to them, "Do not delay me, since the LORD has prospered my way; let me go that I may go to my master." They said, "We will call the maiden, and ask her." And they called Rebekah, and said to her, "Will you go with this man?" She said, "I will go"* (Genesis 24:54-58).

Here is the invitation, an altar call if you please. It climaxes the assault on the will of this girl. It is not an easy choice that she is asked to make. It is revolutionary, disturbing, upsetting. All of her life she has been the protected jewel of that household. She has been kept within the family bosom, cared for, protected and guarded, and now she is asked to go with a man whom she has just met a day or two before, to meet another man who is an utter stranger to her. Yet something about the winsomeness of his appeal, his forthrightness, the glory and attractiveness of what she has heard has won her heart. She is ready to go. We need to recognize that the invitation we give to men and women to become Christians is not an easy choice. It is a revolutionary one. We must clarify the matter and lay it before them: "Will you go?" She said, "I will go."

Finally, in the last scene we see the communion with the son. The work of the Trinity is evident throughout this story. It begins with the command of the Father, proceeds with the cooperation of the Spirit, and ends with the communion with the Son. This is a delightful scene at the end where heart meets heart:

> Now Isaac had come from Beer-lahai-roi, and was dwelling in the Negeb. And Isaac went out to meditate in the field in the evening; and he lifted up his eyes and looked, and behold, there were camels coming. And Rebekah lifted up her eyes, and when she saw Isaac, she alighted from the camel, and said to the servant, "Who is the man yonder, walking in the field to meet us?" The servant said, "It is my master." So she took her veil and covered herself. And the servant told Isaac all the things that he had done. Then Isaac brought her into the tent, and took Rebekah, and she became his wife; and he loved her. So Isaac was comforted after his mother's death (Genesis 24:62-67).

The last words of the servant are here. When Rebekah sees Isaac walking in the field, she says, "Who is this man?" And the servant's words are, "It is my master." This is the place to which we are to bring men and women. The time comes in our own dealing with them when we must stop talking about our personal testimony. We must turn them to look at the one who is winning their hearts and say, "There he is, it's the Master. You deal with him now, talk directly with him."

I think the conversation here when the two met was probably rather stumbling at first. She was very shy and he very reserved. She got off her camel, all atwitter inside. She put her veil over her face so he wouldn't see how she was blushing. This strong, manly young man came up to her and said, "Hello."

She said, "Hello." He said, "Are you Rebekah?" She said, "Yes," and dropped her eyes.

Then he said, "I'm Isaac." (She knew it all the time.) He said, "You can call me Ike."

She said, "Well, my friends call me 'Becky.'" And off they go, hand in hand.

But look at the servant standing by. Can't you imagine him grinning from ear to ear, registering the joy in his heart at the fulfillment of his mission in bringing a bride for Isaac? Doesn't it remind you of those words of John the Baptist when he introduced the Lord Jesus to Israel, and his disciples left him to follow the Lord? Someone asked him how he felt and he said, "He who has the bride is the bridegroom; the friend of the bridegroom, who stands and hears him, rejoices greatly at the bridegroom's voice; therefore this joy of mine is now full. He must increase, but I must decrease" (John 3:29-30).

We are like that servant. We can expect the same brimming of joy in our own hearts as we watch someone join with his Lord in new life. Do you see now that the story of Abraham's servant is your story as well?

A Grand
Finale?

A Matter of Life +

The Joy of L

-sd.

Conclusion
- Ending

2'

19
THE ABUNDANT ENTRANCE

(Genesis 25:1-8)

I suppose it might be proper to begin this last study of Abraham as I sometimes do funerals. Since this is Abraham's funeral, I would say, "We are gathered together to pay our respects to one who has lived among us and has now departed this life." Here is the account of the departure of Abraham. If you have been actively participating in this study of Abraham's life, you must now have a great sense of respect and awe for this "pattern man of faith" as we come to his closing days.

Abraham was called "the friend of God" (James 2:23b), one of the very few men who ever earned that title in the pages of the Bible. He is one of the great universal names of mankind. You can mention the name of Abraham almost any place in the world and they know who he is. There are places where people have never heard of George Washington, or Abraham Lincoln, or Napoleon, but almost every nation and people have heard of Abraham. He is a man of great integrity of heart and purpose, a man of unusual honor and vision, and one of the most faithful men of all time. Yet as we have followed his story through, I hope you have noticed that Abraham is a man of like passions with us. Though we may honor his character and his moral greatness, nevertheless, Scripture clearly shows he has the same make-up as us. As someone has well said, "We are all made of the same mold, but some of us are moldier than others."

Abraham is poured into the same mold that we are. He is capable of lying, deceiving, rebelling, blaming others, loving himself, giving in to weakness, and shutting his eyes to truth. Obviously, here is a man no different from us. Without the grace of God he never would have been any different, just as without the grace of God we could be nothing more than we were in Adam.

What Abraham became by the Spirit is beautifully summarized here in these few verses at the opening of chapter 25. First, his life was abundantly fruitful.

> Abraham took another wife, whose name was Keturah. She bore him Zimran, Jokshan, Medan, Midian, Ishbak, and Shuah. Jokshan was the father of Sheba and Dedan. The sons of Dedan were Asshurim, Letushim, and Leummim. The sons of Midian were Ephah, Epher, Hanoch, Abida, and Eldaah. All these were the children of Keturah (Genesis 25:1-4).

Why are we told this about Abraham in these closing days of his life? Remember that at the very beginning, in the journey out of Ur of the Chaldeans, he
was promised that he would become the father of
many nations. Through Isaac and Ishmael, the two
sons with whom we are most acquainted, several nations arose. Isaac became the father of one group of
nations, and Ishmael of yet another. Through
Keturah, Abraham's second wife, he has six more
sons, each of whom became the founder of other nations. God's promise was literally fulfilled that
Abraham should be the father of many nations and
through him all the nations of the earth would be
blessed.

It is interesting that when Sarah died, Abraham
was about one hundred and forty-seven years old.
After that he took another wife and, remarkably, had
six more sons. We are told specifically in the Scriptures that when Isaac was born, Abraham had long
since ceased to be able to have children. Both he and
Sarah's bodies were dead, their reproductive powers
had ended, and it was by a miracle of grace that Isaac
was born. He was a child of promise and is called the
child of faith.

The writer of Hebrews tells us: "For when God
made a promise to Abraham, since he had no one
greater by whom to swear, he swore by himself, saying, 'Surely I will bless you and multiply you'" (Hebrews 6:13-14). Evidently, when his youthful powers were restored to him in order that he might have
Isaac, they continued afterward and these six other
lads were born to grace his home after Sarah's death.

If we add these six men to Ishmael and Isaac, we
learn that Abraham had a total of eight sons. These
eight sons reveal the fruitfulness of this man's life.

We have noticed how remarkably the Old Testament takes the physical qualities of Abraham's life and makes them picture the spiritual realities in our lives. I have said before that this is one of the most remarkable proofs of the inspiration of the Scripture. It is simply impossible these events could have happened in this way and be such a precise illustration of spiritual truths without the hand of inspiration. You might as well take some book of ancient history and expect to find there an exact picture of spiritual life. This accounting of eight children is a beautiful picture of the fruitfulness of life in the Spirit, life lived by faith as Abraham lived his. You and I, too, can have many sons in this metaphorical sense.

Now to see what I mean, look at 2 Peter 1:3-8, where eight marks of the fruitful life are listed. I wonder if it is mere coincidence that these marks are equal to the number of Abraham's children. I think the following passage could well have been the epitaph of Abraham. His whole life is summarized here for us, beginning with the call of God out of Ur of the Chaldeans unto his own glory and excellence:

> *His divine power has granted to us all things that pertain to life and godliness, through the knowledge of him who called us to his own glory and excellence, by which he has granted to us his precious and very great promises, that through these you may escape from the corruption that is in the world because of passion, and become partakers of the divine nature. For this very reason make every effort to supplement your faith with virtue, and virtue with knowledge, and knowledge with self-control, and self-control with steadfastness, and steadfastness with godliness, and godliness with brotherly*

affection, and brotherly affection with love. For if these things are yours and abound, they keep you from being ineffective or unfruitful in the knowledge of our Lord Jesus Christ (2 Peter 1:3-8).

Peter begins with *faith,* a supreme ingredient of spiritual life. This was the great thing about Abraham; he had confidence in God despite the circumstances. That is a very simple, realistic definition of faith—having confidence in God despite the circumstances—while unbelief is believing the circumstances in spite of God. Which do you have? Faith looks beyond the circumstances when determining an action to be taken. Faith disregards the obstacles, even though they may be disconcerting. Faith believes God despite the circumstances.

This is the basis of all contact with God. You and I cannot be Christians, we cannot live as Christians in any sense, without faith, without believing that God knows what he is talking about. I am eager for our young people to appreciate that the Scriptures are the Word of God. In them, God himself is telling us the truth about life.

We are then told to add *virtue* to faith. In several translations this is rendered "manly courage," or "moral character." I like that. How marvelously we see that in Abraham! With what courage he armed his servants and set out after that great army which came from the east. With what wisdom he surrounded their camp and routed the forces of the enemy, thinking nothing of his own safety in order that he might deliver Lot and the others who had been taken captive! This is one of the key ingredients of a fruitful Christian life. I rejoice that when Jesus Christ came into my life, he came in to make me a man. A Christian is one who begins to demonstrate manliness or womanliness and the courage true humanity reveals.

Then Peter says to add *knowledge* to your virtue, or manly courage. As the old adage has it, there are some people who are so heavenly-minded they have no concern with anything on earth. But it is not like that at all. We need to grow in our knowledge of life. Further, there are some who think Christianity is against knowledge. But the Christian attitude toward knowledge is that all is from God and we are to learn and to comprehend whatever we can. Yet the ultimate secrets of knowledge lie not in any human textbook, but in the book of God. We can find help from many human textbooks, but if we want to get at the streams of life—the very deep things, the basic functions of human life—we will find them only in this book.

Without the Bible we can know neither God nor ourselves. We are the greatest enigma of the universe. The Spirit of God at work is always the spirit of knowledge, teaching us basic facts about God and man which can never be learned in any university of secular knowledge.

Then there is *self-control*. Abraham was able to keep his temper amid the irritations of those around him. He showed a wonderful degree of self-control. Now there is a type of self- control that says, "Just wait, my time is coming. I won't say anything now, but just you wait—we'll straighten things out later!" But this is not what the Spirit produces. Spirit given self-control says: "Before you speak in irritation, remember that you belong to God; he is the Lord of your life, and what you say must reflect him." God-control results in self-control.

Hudson Taylor once described an incident when, since he could get no other transportation, he chartered a small boat to take him down river to an appointment. While he was waiting at the wharf to board, a very richly dressed mandarin, a Chinese teacher, came to the wharf with a couple of men following him. Seeing this little boat there, he asked the driver, "Where are you going?" The man told him and the mandarin said, "I want the boat." The owner tried to explain to him that the boat had already been chartered. The mandarin asked, "To whom did you charter it?" The man said, "To this foreigner," pointing to Hudson.

The mandarin looked at him arrogantly and with a wave of disdain swept him aside and said, "I'll take the boat!" Hudson Taylor said he could feel the ire rise within him. The mandarin was standing between him and the river, and all he would have to do was push and the man would land in the river. He started to do it when he felt the restraint of the Spirit. Turning to the man, he said, "I know you regard me as nothing but a white foreign devil, but I have chartered this boat and it is mine by right. The Jesus that is in me kept me from pushing you into the river just now. You richly deserve that, but the Lord kept me from it because he has not sent me here to push Chinese people into the river, but to win them for Christ. The boat is mine and I must take it; however, I invite you to come along with me and be my guest." Rather confused and amazed, the mandarin accepted his invitation and went aboard, and they had a wonderful conversation all the way to their destination.

To self-control we are to add *steadfastness*, which is an old fashioned word for patience. And what a word that is! Have you ever noticed that God cannot give patience? He can only teach it. There is no use praying for patience. If you do, the Lord will send you tribulation, because "tribulation worketh patience" (Romans 5:3, KJV). So watch out. You need patience, but it can't be given; it can only be taught.

What a marvelous manifestation of the Spirit this is! Look back at old Abraham waiting twenty-five years for a son. The promise had been given, but he waited for twenty-five long, weary years before that promise was fulfilled. You can see something of what the Spirit of God taught this man in the way of patience. Most of us are like the little girl who banged her cup on her highchair and demanded milk. Her mother told her to be patient. She said, "I've got patience, but I don't have any milk."

To patience or steadfastness, add *godliness*. What is this? It is simply sensing the presence of God in your daily life. Abraham was the man with the tent and the altar. He built an altar everywhere he went. He was an intimate friend of God. He *knew* God; this is what godliness is. In the New Testament it is expressed in the phrase, "Whatever you do, do all to the glory of God" (1 Corinthians 10:31b). Godliness is a consciousness of his presence.

To godliness add *brotherly affection*. This is the sharing of self in hospitality and by encouraging one another, inviting someone over for dinner just to give him a word of encouragement and to strengthen him. This is a practical demonstration of the Spirit at work.

Last, we are to add *love*. Love is the most unmistakable fruit of the Spirit. First Corinthians 13 is the commentary on what love really is, and this kind of love is produced only by the Spirit!

This is the truly fruitful life, suggested by

Abraham's eight sons. These eight beautiful virtues are part of the Spirit-filled life. Peter continues,

> *For if these things are yours and abound, they keep you from being ineffective or unfruitful in the knowledge of our Lord Jesus Christ. For whoever lacks these things is blind and shortsighted and has forgotten that he was cleansed from his old sins. Therefore, brethren, be the more zealous to confirm your call and election, for if you do this you will never fall; so there will be richly provided for you an entrance into the eternal kingdom of our Lord and Savior Jesus Christ.*

Abraham has now come, at the close of his life, to this abundant entrance into the kingdom of the Father.

In Genesis 25, we learn that not only was Abraham's life abundantly fruitful, but the next few verses make it clear that his was also a life of practical foresight:

> *Abraham gave all he had to Isaac. But to the sons of his concubines Abraham gave gifts, and while he was still living he sent them away from his son Isaac, eastward to the east country (Genesis 25:5,6).*

Abraham never forgot that Isaac was the son of promise and the divinely chosen heir. He was constantly alert to protect the inheritance of God. He anticipated danger and made provision for his other sons so that they would not destroy what God was doing in Isaac's life. Isaac is throughout a picture of Christ. We read that Abraham gave all that he had to Isaac, just as the Father gives all that he has to the Son. This is a portrait of a life that is so Christ-centered that it exercises care to protect the inheritance and to keep away the things that might harm it.

This expression, "He sent them . . . eastward to the east country" is significant. When Abraham first came into the land, he pitched his tent between Ai and Bethel, with Ai on the east and Bethel on the west. Ai means ruin; Bethel means the house or place of God. Isaac was given the inheritance in the west, in the place of God, while the other sons were sent out into the east countries to the place of ruin. This ruin is a picture of the natural life, the life that we had from Adam.

As with Abraham, we are expected to show practical foresight. Just as Abraham sent these sons away so they would not injure the inheritance given to Isaac, so we are to be careful not to get into situations that threaten our spiritual lives.

When I was a young man in Montana, I heard of a cowboy who came in from the country every weekend. He would tie his horse up in front of the saloon, go in and get drunk. Then one day he was converted in a little church there, stopped drinking completely and became a godly man. For a long time after that, though, he kept tying his horse to the hitching rack in front of the saloon.

One day an older Christian took him aside and said to him, "Now son, I know you never go into the saloon anymore, and I notice you are always at prayer meeting and your life is a blessing to many. But I would like to give you one suggestion. Change your hitching post. Sooner or later you are going to be tempted to go back into that place. Why don't you just hitch your horse down the street a few doors so you won't have to walk past the saloon?" That is good advice. Change your hitching post. Take practical foresight to protect your spiritual life. It is a wise course for all who are true sons of Abraham.

Abraham's life was also a full one:

> *These are the days of the years of Abraham's life, a hundred and seventy-five years. Abraham breathed his last and died in a good old age, an old man and full of years, and was gathered to his people (Genesis 25:7,8).*

If you and I had been with Abraham at the moments of decision in his life, we might often have pitied him. When he left Ur, we might have said, "Abraham, you poor fool, do you mean you are going to wander out there in the desert and perhaps live in a tent the rest of your life, when you could have enjoyed the city and all of its blessings?"

When he allowed Lot to choose the best of the land, perhaps some of us might have thought, "Abraham, don't throw away your rights like that! You are the oldest one. You have the right to choose. Why let Lot take that choice piece while you are left with this dry old pasture? You are throwing away your rights." Abraham let Lot choose, and God chose for him.

And do you remember when the king of Sodom offered all the riches of Sodom to Abraham, Abraham said, "I'll not take even one of your shoelaces, I don't want any of it." Some us us would have been tempted to say, "Now wait, Abraham, you are carrying this a little too far. You could have deducted this from your income tax; and just think what you are missing, all the riches of Sodom you could have. Think how you could use it in the Lord's work!" But Abraham chose God every time, and his was a life of fullness.

He lived one hundred and seventy-five years, and every one was packed full, spiced with excitement and adventure, filled with challenge and interest, rich in faith and blessing. He died an old man, full of days. How true are our Lord's words in Mark 10: "Truly, I say to you, there is no one who has left house or brothers or sisters or mother or father or children or lands, for my sake and for the gospel, who will not receive a hundredfold *now in this time*, houses and brothers and sisters and mothers and children and lands, with persecutions, and in the age to come eternal life" (Mark 10:29,30). That is the promise of a full life to those who live in the Spirit.

In verse 8 there is an indication that our pattern man of faith enjoyed divine fellowship: he "was gathered to his people." That does not refer to his body, because Abraham was not buried back in Ur with the rest of his family. Nor does it refer to the fact that he was to enter into the realm of death where the rest of his family had gone. We are told Abraham was an idolater in his early years, and his family worshiped idols. They were not, therefore, godly men, and Abraham was not gathered to them.

The account says that he was gathered to "his people." What does that mean? It means that he was gathered to those before him who had exercised faith in God. He was with those righteous ones who all through that intervening history had been walking with God. Enoch and Noah were examples of such men who learned to know the living God. Those are Abraham's people. Just as the people who are ours are not the fleshly people, but the ones to whom we are spiritually bound. Perhaps this is what our Lord Jesus meant when word came to him that his mother and his brothers were waiting outside, and he refused to go, saying to those with him, "Here are my mother and my brothers! Whoever does the will of God is my brother, and sister, and mother" (Mark 3:34b-35).

So Abraham was gathered to "his people," as we may be as well.

This phrase indicates that by no means did his life end 4,000 years ago. When the Sadducees—who did not believe in the resurrection of the dead—asked Jesus a question, he answered them: "Have you not read what was said to you by God, 'I am the God of Abraham, and the God of Isaac, and the God of Jacob?' He is not God of the dead, but of the living" (Matthew 22:31b-32). Thus he answered those who did not believe in life after death. He was saying that Abraham is yet living. God is the God of the living, not of the dead! On another occasion, looking forward into the future, he said, "I tell you, many will come from east and west and sit at table with Abraham, Isaac, and Jacob in the kingdom of heaven" (Matthew 8:11).

We also have that amazing story in Luke 16 in which our Lord tells of the rich man and Lazarus. Lazarus died and was carried to Abraham's bosom, the place of fellowship where Abraham was with God the Father. The rich man in Hades, seeing him there, begged him to send someone to relieve his torment and the anguish of his soul. And Abraham said, "They have Moses and the prophets; let them hear them. If they do not hear Moses and the prophets, neither will they be convinced if some one should rise from the dead" (Luke 16:29,31).

In these many ways Abraham's life pictures yours and mine. There was nothing unusual about him; nevertheless God made him an extraordinary person, whose life reaches far beyond the realms of earth into eternity. His life is one of blessing, fellowship, and fullness. Abraham stands as a living testimony to anyone who takes the path of faith and walks this way. In so living, we, too, will find the same blessing. The author of Hebrews, in the great "heroes of faith" chapter, has this to say about Abraham and others before him:

> *These all died in faith, not having received what was promised, but having seen it and greeted it from afar, and having acknowledged that they were strangers and exiles on the earth. For people who speak thus make it clear that they are seeking a homeland. If they had been thinking of that land from which they had gone out, they would have had opportunity to return. But as it is, they desire a better country, that is, a heavenly one. Therefore God is not ashamed to be called their God, for he has prepared for them a city (Hebrews 11:13-16).*

Abraham's life is the life of every Christian, for all who walk in faith with Jesus Christ are called to be his, to be possessed of him, to live as pilgrims and strangers on earth. The fruitfulness we desire and the abundant life in the everlasting kingdom of the Father will be fulfilled in us . . . just as they were in the life of Abraham.